Conversations with 50 inspiring people

COMPILED AND EDITED BY HAL DONALDSON,
KEN HORN, SCOTT HARRUP AND ASHLI O'CONNELL

Heather,
God bless you richly!
Ken Horn
John M Kennedy

PENTECOSTAL EVANGEL BOOKS

GOSPEL PUBLISHING HOUSE
Springfield, MO. 65802-1894
www.GospelPublishing.com

In loving memory of Ralph W. Harris.

Special recognition to the staff of *Today's Pentecostal Evangel:* Connie Cross, Jodi Harmon, John W. Kennedy, Matt Key, Ron Kopczick, Marc McBride, Kirk Noonan, Isaac Olivarez and Jena Schaumburg.

Cover design by Matt Key

Cover photos: (top row, left to right) Lisa Whelchel, Pat Boone, Cris Carter, Rebecca St. James, Dr. David Yonggi Cho; (bottom row, left to right) Nicky Cruz, Terry Meeuwsen, Dallas Holm, Debby Boone (photo by CharlesBush.com), Admiral Vern E. Clark; (back cover) Napoleon Kaufman

Library of Congress Control Number 2004106305
International Standard Book Number 0-88243-325-3
Printed in the United States of America

Introduction

Today's Pentecostal Evangel has interviewed thousands of engaging individuals with compelling stories. This has made the "Conversation" section one of the most popular features in the magazine.

The interviews have featured pastors, celebrities and laypeople; mature believers and new Christians; people in ministry and show business; blue collar workers, white collar workers and homemakers. All have had something significant to say to the body of Christ. This book contains 50 of the most popular interviews from the pages of *Today's Pentecostal Evangel.* May these conversations provide encouragement, insight and inspiration.

— *Today's Pentecostal Evangel* staff

Note: The name of the interviewer can be found at the end of each interview.

Contents

Foreword

A number of years ago I was sitting high up on a mountain in Colorado. At approximately 10,000 feet, the view was breathtaking. It was a cool, clear morning in November, and the exhilaration of both the view and the slight chill in the air made me feel incredibly alive.

I gazed across a vast expanse of smaller hills, rough canyons and broad meadows to a mountain range very far off. I tried to guess how far away this seemingly even taller mountain range was. That evening I learned that my guess of 50 miles was not even half the distance, as the farther range was nearly 150 miles away.

Sometime later, as my wife was struggling with cancer, I included this mountaintop experience in a song entitled "Heal Me."

I've stood upon the mountain and looked across to higher peaks and more.

But the only way to reach them is to journey through the lowly valley floor.

As I continued to soak in God's beauty from my 10,000-foot vantage point, something quite extraordinary happened that I will never forget. A thick bank of clouds suddenly moved in at about 9,000 feet, virtually causing everything below me to disappear. All that was left to see was a range of snow-covered mountains 150 miles away.

I thought how incredible it would be to walk across the top of this white carpet of clouds to the distant mountains. In a world of fantasy it would be an easy, fun journey. In reality, I knew that the only way to arrive at that other mountaintop was to travel difficult days through rough canyons, across roaring rapids and through dark forests.

So it is in life. God, in His great mercy and grace, allows us the occasional mountaintop experiences. But they are the exception, not the rule. Most of life is lived in deep valleys, rough canyons and sometimes seemingly endless fields, often under a thick blanket of clouds.

This book shares the journey of some of God's choicest servants as they have followed God's pathway through the rough terrain of life, finding His grace more than sufficient at every step.

May you rejoice in God's faithfulness, may you feel the strength of His guiding hand and may you take joy in the journey knowing that the final destination will be the ultimate mountaintop experience.

Your fellow traveler,
Dallas Holm

Emilie Barnes
Living an organized life

*For more than 20 years noted author and home-and-office organization expert **Emilie Barnes** has been speaking to women on how to get organized and simplify their lives. She is the author of more than 60 books and the co-author of six cookbooks.*

Q: **You write books on organization. How can I become better organized?**

Start with a teachable spirit, because then you have a heart to learn. Set a plan. We look at the total picture and get stressed because we don't have time. Set a timer for 15 minutes and start with what is stressing you out the most in your home. Do the worst first. Stop when the timer goes off — even if the job isn't complete — and work on it again tomorrow.

Q: **You hold More Hours in My Day time-management seminars. What are some of the rewards?**

I was raised in a Jewish home. My father passed away and my mother opened a little dress shop. She taught me washing, ironing, planning and shopping for meals, and how to sew. God took the things Momma taught me and built a ministry from them.

When Bob and I began to date, he introduced me to the Lord. We married young. At age 20 we had our first child, and I discovered I was pregnant again shortly after my brother's three children came to live with us. We had five children under the age of 5. How was I going to handle that without organization?

When the children went off to college, this ministry was dropped in my lap. I was having a Bible study in my home. The women told me, "We come to your home and you've got dinner in the oven, muffins in a basket, coffee and tea for us, and it's only 9:30. How do you do it?"

That was the beginning. My Bible study group invited their neighbors and soon we couldn't get everybody in the house. I started accepting invitations to go to churches, and in 1982 I wrote my first book, *More Hours in My Day.*

Q: As you travel, what's the most-asked question?

Today's women are saying, "I need more hours in my day." They feel overwhelmed. They've got the home, husband, children, church, job, and maybe they're homeschooling as well. I suggest they go back to the plan. Take that 15 minutes and begin to relieve some stress. Eighty-five percent of our stresses are caused by disorganization.

Q: How can I get my family involved helping me?

Have a family meeting. Mom goes into the meeting with her list of things she needs help with. Get suggestions from them how they can help. Hand everybody a 3-by-5 card with the motto, "Don't put it down; put it away." Tell them to post it where they can see it.

Q: You mention priorities. How does that relate to organizing our lives and homes?

Our number one priority should be our relationship with God. I've written a devotional book called *Fifteen Minutes Alone with God.* If we will take 15 minutes a day and go into our prayer closets, we'll come out new women. We will be able to draw from that power throughout the day.

We make appointments to see the doctor, dentist, or our child's teacher. We wouldn't think of not keeping those appointments. Keeping our daily appointments with our Heavenly Father is priority one. Our second priority is our husband, our third is our children, and our fourth is our home.

God redeems time spent with Him. It will come back to us many times.

Q: What advice do you have for those who feel too busy?

Seek first the kingdom of God. Even though you are busy with hectic schedules, there's hope. When you put God first, He gives you a promise that He will take care of the rest. You can run a home that has balance to it.

— *Belinda Conway*

Anne Beiler
God has a plan

Anne Beiler started selling hand-rolled soft pretzels at a farmer's market in Downingtown, Pa., in 1988. Beiler and her husband, Jonas, both Spirit-filled believers, opened the farmer's market stand to supplement their income while Jonas provided free counseling in the Lancaster County community in which they had both been raised. The dream for a counseling center was fulfilled in 1992, just three years prior to Auntie Anne's Hand-Rolled Soft Pretzels going international. In 16 years, the company grew from one pretzel store to more than 800 locations worldwide. Beiler credits her focus on people and her faith in God for Auntie Anne's success. In part, the company mission statement reads, "We strive to make everything we do pay tribute to God who has entrusted us with this task."

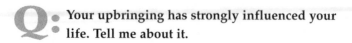

Q: **Your upbringing has strongly influenced your life. Tell me about it.**

I grew up in Lancaster County, Pa., on a farm with five brothers and two sisters. My parents were Amish. We had a horse and buggy and no electricity until I was almost 3. When we joined an Amish Mennonite church we could have a black car and electricity and tractors on the farm. Mom and Dad provided for us very well and took us to church every Sunday and taught us obedience to God and the fear of God. Jonas and I were married in the Mennonite church when I was 19 and he was 21. We later received the baptism in the Holy Spirit, which changed our lives tremendously.

Q: Tell me about that experience.

I went to a women's Bible study and Jo Ton, a woman from Indonesia, gave her testimony. She said to me, "Have you heard of being filled with the Holy Spirit?" I was 21 when I received the Baptism. My husband, my two sisters, their husbands and then my whole family experienced the infilling of the Holy Spirit. The baptism in the Holy Spirit brought me into a relationship with Christ I had never experienced before.

Q: Tell me about your children.

LaWonna and LaVale have made us grandparents. Our middle daughter, Angie, died as a baby. Angie's death began a journey that was profound and also very difficult for Jonas and me.

Q: What happened to Angie?

She was run over by a farm tractor when she was 19 months old. Had it not been for God's grace and mercy, and the wonderful godly husband who loved me as Christ loves him, I never would have climbed out of depression. I believe Angela was sent to me and my family for many reasons, but a key purpose was for me to become the kind of person that Christ wants me to be. I experienced emotional pain, anguish of soul and deep depression as a result of her death.

Q: Out of your ordeal Jonas wanted to start a counseling center. That's what prompted you to start Auntie Anne's. Did you have immediate success or were there doubts along the way?

Our success came only after Jonas added his ingredients to our existing pretzel recipe. The first tray out of the oven was an instant success. People would take a bite of the pretzel, stop, and then look at the pretzel in amazement. Soon we were doing about 1,500 pretzels a day, and the lines were long. An Amish girl, about 18 years old, kept telling us we should go to the Harrisburg market. I went to look at Harrisburg and that's where we started the second store. I had a lot of fear, but God clearly said to me, "Fear not, for I am blessing you."

I said, "OK, Lord, then I'll take You at Your Word." We built nine stores in 1989. From 1990–95 we worked on our corporate infrastructure.

The spiritual aspect of it was so powerful. I didn't have high school or college degrees, so I had to rely on the Word of God. I dug into the Book of Proverbs and we based and built our business on its principles. God encouraged me along the way. I remember in June 1990, I was sitting in a church service on missions Sunday, and I saw myself rolling pretzels and Jesus standing there. It wasn't a vision; it was just a clear impression from the Lord. Jesus spoke to my heart and said, "I want you to use Auntie Anne's as a vehicle for missions." There was a big smile on His face and I understood clearly for the first time God's purpose for Auntie Anne's. I knew I was to put everything I had into Auntie Anne's and Jonas was to do the counseling part. We both understood clearly what our roles were. Along the way, God has totally directed us.

Q: What advice would you give to people, women in particular, who want to pursue a business dream?

I don't push my way into places simply because I'm a woman. As a woman of God, if I find my place in Christ, I don't have to be pushy and make my own way, but rather, God simply opens doors and I walk through them. It's the same with a man. We make too big a deal out of genders. If you like who you are in God, then everywhere you go you'll be comfortable. When I realized that God called me to this, I was out of my comfort zone. But God helped me to become comfortable with myself first and then He helped me to be comfortable with His call on my life. With God, I can go anywhere and nothing intimidates me.

Q: Do you think that a lot of people never pursue a God-given dream because it's out of their comfort zone?

If you stay frozen in fear, you will never accomplish what God wants you to accomplish. There were times when I was emotionally and physically overcome by fear. The Psalmist says, "When I am afraid, I will trust in you" (Psalm 56:3). It's OK to be afraid, but you can't stay there. God is patient with us and He comforts us. Every time I saw a door opened to me, faith would say, "Go through the door," and as I did I saw that God had gone before me.

Q: How have your core values contributed to your success?

They are the reason we're successful, even though they require sacrifice at times. People who came to us — franchisees and employees — in the early days knew nothing about the franchising industry. We knew very little ourselves, but we learned together. During the first 3–5 years we actually bought equipment back and paid off some franchisees' loans. Our accountant told us we shouldn't do that. But I had to sleep at night. If you do what is right and go the second mile for people, God will bless you.

Consistently solid ethics are vital in business. If you say you're going to call someone back today, then do it. If you say you can't do a deal, don't make up stories. Always tell the truth. Simply telling the truth is probably the most impacting principle of Auntie Anne's.

Q: What are your core values in giving and tithing?

The Bible says to give with good measure, pressed down, shaken together and overflowing. The measure in which you give is the same measure God uses to bless you. More specifically, I've found that tithing brought about a dimension of giving in my life that started the incredible journey of blessing. For the work of Christ to be completed requires money. Tithing is something everybody can do.

Q: So, when people buy Auntie Anne's pretzels part of that is giving back to God's work?

Yes. A percentage of our profits goes to the Family Information Center, which is a center for hurting families. There are many opportunities for us as a company. I believe God has greater things in store, and it's all about the work of the Kingdom.

Q: Tell me about prayer in your company.

Every Monday we have prayer time, and we also pray before all of our business meetings.

Q: What brings you joy and satisfaction?

Giving and watching people grow — professionally, spiritually and emotionally.

Q: How do you maintain a spirit of humility and stay grounded?

I know where I came from, and I keep looking back to remember. I'm a country girl from the farm. I know what it's like to work hard. I've experienced plenty of pain and things in my life that have been unpleasant and I know that God is my Source. I stay focused on Him and He keeps taking me places where I'm forced to depend on Him for my every need — emotionally, spiritually and for wisdom.

Q: Anything else?

God has a plan for our lives. We can have confidence in Him that He will take us where He wants us to go. We don't have to become fearful and wonder what God's will is. It will come to us and unfold over time. We need to trust Him for our futures. Each day we must do what is at hand and be faithful in the little things.

— Hal Donaldson

Raymond Berry
More to life than football

*Hall of Famer **Raymond Berry** played for the Baltimore Colts from 1955–67. He led the NFL in numerous statistical categories, retiring as the NFL's all-time leading receiver through 1967. His 12 receptions and 178 yards helped the Colts win the 1958 NFL Championship Game over the New York Giants. As head coach of the New England Patriots, he guided them to an appearance in Super Bowl XX. Today, Berry speaks extensively to both Christian groups and secular audiences.*

 How did you come to Christ?

I had been playing in the NFL for about four or five years for the Baltimore Colts. We played in New York for the World Championship against the New York Giants. It was an overtime game that we managed to win. At that point in my life I didn't really give God much thought. But after the game I had an awareness of God that was totally unexpected. I began to understand that my athletic ability was a gift. The opportunity to use it was a gift. The question I had was,

Why? There had to be more to life than chasing a football.

My friend and teammate Don Shinnick began to talk to me about Christ. I asked him once, "How do you go about doing this, Don?" He told me what to say, and I prayed and said, "God, I'm going to trust Your Son Jesus Christ as my Savior, and I mean business about this. But I don't really know what I'm doing." And that is about all I said. And that's all I meant to say. Before that, I had never had any peace in my life. I really struggled with guilt. After I prayed and asked Christ to be my Savior, I experienced peace. I began to realize that I had been forgiven. My whole life changed. I began to get answers for my questions. I began to understand that God had a purpose for me. He had a plan for my life. For the last 40 years I have been finding out what that plan is.

Q: How did your Christian walk progress?

I had also questioned what would happen to me when I die. I started reading the New Testament and found a tremendous amount of Scripture that deals with eternal life. I gradually realized that eternal life is a gift that God gives believers. It is based on His love for us, and on what Christ did. It is not based on anything we can do. That is what grace is. You're saved by grace and not works. That was a tremendous revelation to fully understand and have assurance that I knew where I was going to spend eternity. And it had nothing to do with my being able to earn it. It was all about mercy.

I was also searching for the purpose of life. I began to realize that the Scriptures were pointing to the purpose in life as doing the will of God. Don had told me the night he led me to Christ, "Raymond, you don't have the power to live a Christian life. If you will trust Christ, He will come and live in you. He's the power to live it. Your job is to let Him." I began to understand that the purpose of the Christian life is to do the will of God. I began to realize God gave me power to do His will through the Holy Spirit. I could see that in my own strength I could not do what God wanted me to do. I just had to learn to yield, submit and obey. It was encouraging to know that I could accomplish what God wanted me to do because He gave me the power to do it.

Q: Were there challenges in living a Christian life while you were in the NFL?

I found the challenge in the Christian life was letting Jesus be Lord. As I began to study the New Testament, I began to see that man without God's help is unable to live a life that pleases God. God sent Christ to the cross to pay for our sins and satisfy His justice. But His plan included giving us power to live a Christian life through the indwelling Christ. Christ really comes to live in the Christian. He is the power to love people, to forgive people, to carry out God's will and plan for us. It is power we don't have. We are not designed to have the power ourselves, we are designed to have Christ's power in us and to submit and yield to Him. That's a daily step-by-step process.

Q: Would you talk about the importance of the Word of God?

As a professional football player I had a rhythm of six months on the job and six months off-season. It gave me a tremendous opportunity for in-depth Scripture study. For the first five or six years that I was a Christian I studied a lot of New Testament Scriptures. I wrote a lot of Scriptures out on index cards. I would take them with me in the car and review. I really wasn't consciously memorizing them, but I was ingraining the Word of God into my mind and beginning to actually commit many of them to memory. Today when I study Scripture, I really like to write my studies down. I walk two or three miles several times a week, and I will take those Scriptures with me while I'm walking and look at them and meditate on them. I have experienced the power of the Word of God. I've seen it work in the lives of people and have great confidence in delivering any message to an audience if the Word is in it. I know that the Word is going to do its work whether or not they remember one thing I say.

Q: **Did you find many other Christians in the NFL when you were playing?**

I became a Christian in 1960. I wasn't really aware of it at the time, but I can now see that four to five years prior to that God really began to work in the NFL. People in the NFL were becoming Christians. Men were being called to minister to professional athletes and present Christ and help them grow. All of a sudden there were a lot of guys coming to know the Lord in the NFL and in professional baseball.

Q: **You also coached in the NFL. Describe that experience.**

I never really cared that much about coaching when I finished playing. But in seeking God's direction in what He wanted me to do, I realized that He wanted me to coach. I had the assurance that God called me to coach and He would give me the ability. During 20 years of coaching, I saw miraculous things. I also went through tremendous trials, disappointments, heartaches, persecutions and attacks. It wasn't a bed of roses. But God was faithful in sustaining me and enabling me in a whole lot of victories. I'm talking spiritual victories as well as victories on the field. I grew as a Christian through having to really trust the Lord. I gradually realized that God was enabling me to stay in a position of humility so that He could work His work and that I wouldn't get in His way. I began to understand that I could be thankful when I felt inadequate.

Q: **How did it feel when you became a member of the Hall of Fame?**

When I retired, I knew that my statistical numbers would qualify me for the Hall. The numbers just say that. But it made me more aware that the only reason it happened was because God intended for it to. I knew enough about my abilities and capabilities to know by all rights it should never have happened. But God overcame a lot of things and He used me. When God creates influence, He has a reason. It's not for my glory or my enjoyment. It's for God's glory and His purposes inevitably. He is interested in ministering to people and bringing people to Christ. He has given me influence so I can be a witness for Him.

Q: Anything else?

I stand on Jeremiah 9:23,24: "Let not the wise man glory in his wisdom, let not the mighty man glory in his might, nor let the rich man glory in his riches; but let him who glories glory in this, that he understands and knows Me, that I am the Lord" (NKJV). In this passage God tells us where life is and where it is not. God's priority is that we have a relationship with Him. I found a relationship with God more than 40 years ago and it is still going on.

— *Ken Horn*

Debby Boone
Making a happy home

Debby Boone has spent a career in the entertainment industry, singing, acting and writing children's books with her husband, Gabriel Ferrer, who is a minister. But her primary occupation has been raising four children.

Q: **You do so many things, from singing to acting to raising children. Is there one you enjoy the most?**

I feel incredibly blessed to be fulfilled in all of them. There is nothing like expressing yourself creatively when you are a creative person and having people respond. But there is the same joy in watching your kids excel. It is hard to keep a balance, and I don't think I always have. I feel blessed to be in a good relationship with my husband who brings a balance to our home. We are so different, yet our strengths and weaknesses balance out. I see my kids are growing up in a happy home.

Early on, when I would travel, my husband stayed home with the children. Now it's more difficult with both of us working and having three teenage girls at home. I'm saying no to things I would normally say yes to, because I know that teenage girls need at least one of their parents around paying close attention. It's always a juggling act. The only way any of it has made sense is in praying and seeking the guidance of the Lord.

Q: What is your family schedule like?

There is no routine schedule, which is part of the difficulty and what I long for. One of my goals is to get a regular job on a family television show so that I have a schedule. The majority of the work I do takes me away from home.

Q: What's the best advice anyone gave you about being a mother?

Someone said that if your kids are growing up in a loving home, that compensates for a lot of mistakes. I'm seeing the fruits of that. I don't consider myself the perfect mother. It's the biggest source of guilt in my life, feeling like I didn't handle a situation right. I have a son in college in Boston. I'm always wondering if he's OK. Every parent walks that fine line between wanting to shelter their children and knowing that, if they want their children to be whole, healthy human beings, they have to let them go.

Q: What encouragement can you give to working moms?

Rather than wasting time and energy on guilt, use it to tell your kids how much you love them and how proud you are of them. Talk about your dreams for them and how they bring you joy. That will always be a better expenditure of time and energy than wishing you had done something better.

Q: How do you stay close to God?

The most important thing is knowing that my life falls apart if I don't put aside time to pray and read and nourish myself on a spiritual level. This morning I finished my time literally in my closet. I have this great closet that was designed with a stained-glass bay window in it. It is the place I go to read and to pray when my kids go to school. I can see right outside. All my books and journals and the things that create this spiritual place for me are there. It has become a lifeline for me. That's where I quiet myself and lay all my anxieties down. My faith grows and I know that life isn't just happening to me, but I'm really partnering with God. It certainly makes me feel that I have more to contribute, whether it's something my kids are going through, or my responsibilities as a mother and wife, or career decisions. I realize I am not the one who has to be in control and make it all happen. I trust that all my needs are met in Him.

— *Joel Kilpatrick*

Pat Boone
Teen Challenge, Hollywood and patriotism

Pat Boone is a Grammy-winning recording artist, star of stage, screen and television, and entrepreneur. At one time a Top 10 box office draw, he has also hosted Gospel America, *a gospel music TV program, and currently hosts a syndicated music radio program. Boone has been an elder at The Church on the Way in Van Nuys, Calif., for 35-plus years.*

Q: **You've had a wide-ranging career in entertainment over the years, but many people remember you for one movie role in particular — that of David Wilkerson in the film adaptation of *The Cross and the Switchblade*. How did you come in contact with the book and the movie?**

I was on my way to Mexico City and at the airport I picked up a paperback copy of *The Cross and the Switchblade*. I was curious how they combined those two images in the title. I started reading it on the plane and by about page 31 or 32 I was getting goose bumps. I kept asking myself if this was supposed to be a true story. David Wilkerson was detailing an absolute miracle that happened on the streets of New York City. I'd been taught in my church background that God doesn't do miracles anymore. I couldn't put it down.

When I got back to L.A., I called David Wilkerson in New York. I'd never met him. I said, "I'm Pat Boone, the entertainer," and I started to explain. "I read your book. Did all these things you talk about really happen just that way? ... I really think there ought to be a movie made of this book. I think it would be a very successful film."

He was less than enthusiastic. He told me he thought Hollywood would twist the story around. Then, all of a sudden, he began to pray about it over the phone. "Lord," he prayed, "my life's Your life, my story's Your story, and if You want anything made of this, then You do it. You know Pat Boone; I don't. You know whether he should be part of it."

God put the pieces together and did a wonderful work in my life. By the time we started filming, I had been baptized in the Holy Spirit.

Q: Did you face any challenges in making the film?

I'd get in a cab in mid-town Manhattan to go deep into Harlem for the day's shooting, and the cab driver would say, "You want to go where? That's a dangerous neighborhood, man." I'd give him his fare as we got close to the day's location and he would only slow down enough for me to open the door and hop out and he was out of there.

When we filmed, we went into the very streets, alleys and basements where the story had been lived. I felt very inadequate to play David, but I prayed continually and I knew God was doing something. After we had been filming a few days, David came on the set in a basement in Harlem. Then he went to see some of the film we had shot the day before.

After they rolled the shots, the lights came up. David looked at me and said, "You're starting to look like me." Right then, I knew the Holy Spirit was doing something. The film became the most successful independently produced and distributed film ever up to then.

Q: **The movie has continued to be a blessing over the years.**

It never got the kind of big splash on neighborhood screens that it should have had. But *The Cross and the Switchblade* has been translated into 15 to 20 languages. I've had people from Iran and Iraq tell me they've seen the film in their language. Those countries consider it an anti-drug film. Even with its strong Christian message it is still seen around the world in all these languages and even in Muslim countries.

They're looking for something that will discourage drug use, and this film does it.

Q: **How did you come to know Christ?**

Well, thank God I was born not only in America, but to Christian parents. A lot of us have had those blessings, and we take them for granted.

Dad was a building contractor and Mom was a registered nurse. I was their first child followed fairly quickly in the next six years by a brother and two sisters. My parents were very serious about church attendance and involvement. I sat with my parents on the front row or no farther back than the second row for all of my growing up days. We went to Sunday morning service, Sunday night and Wednesday night. We tried to go to every revival service. Plus we had Bible reading and prayer and devotionals at home. Even though it got tiring to us kids at times, we realized that church was as important to our parents as eating, sleeping or anything else. When I was 13, I confessed Jesus Christ as my Savior and was baptized in water.

I asked my parents if I could have the unfinished attic as my bedroom. So Mom and Dad let me have a bed upstairs among all the boxes and clothes and all the paraphernalia that six people in a family collect. And that was a precious place to me. I remember many, many times on my knees, looking out the window of the attic into the side yard and up the street and asking the Lord to use my life, and to use me.

Q: **How did God begin to direct you?**

I loved singing. I sang at every honorable opportunity. I turned down opportunities to sing with dance bands and supper clubs because of my faith. Because of the invitations I turned down, I started to think there was no chance for me to be a professional singer. I'd pray about it when I was milking the family cow, Rosemary. I would talk to the Lord and say, "I wish I could be a singer like Julius LaRosa on *Arthur Godfrey and His Friends.*" You know, within about two years of those prayers, I was a regular on the show. I was at school at Columbia University, married to Shirley, my high school sweetheart, and I was a father. God just had His hand on me.

Q: **Not many people realize you were also involved in ministry during your early singing career.**

When I first went to college I was preparing to be a teacher. I was preaching in a little country church in Slidell, Texas. They had students come preach for them because they couldn't afford a regular preacher. There were only about 30 or 40 people out in this rural area. For months I was their regular preacher while I was at school at North Texas State.

While I was on *Arthur Godfrey and His Friends* and fulfilling my recording contract, I was enrolled in Columbia. I became the song leader and Sunday School teacher at a little church in Manhattan. I was in college and having kids and living over in New Jersey and starting my own weekly television show for Chevrolet and making some movies for 20th Century Fox. But every Sunday and Sunday night, just like when I grew up, I was at that little congregation in Manhattan.

Q: You're known as both an outspoken Christian and successful entertainer and celebrity. How do you balance those roles?

I didn't always balance them that well. In the beginning, I had a very special sense of God's miraculous provision. I remember turning down a role that I thought would compromise my testimony, even though I can look back now and see that it was an honorable role. I made some people very angry. Little did any of us know that my turning that role down would lead to my doing *Journey to the Center of the Earth*. I did what I thought God wanted me to do, and He honored that.

But my reputation made people think I was too good to be commercial, and a kind of squeaky-clean image grew. And I started to chafe at that. I made concessions and I did things I didn't think were right and gradually I sold out more and more until I nearly lost marriage, family, reputation ... everything. I wrote about it all in my book *A New Song*. All the crumbling and caving in to pressures brought me to a new commitment and a realization — I could not work out my own salvation with fear and trembling. We read Philippians 2:12, "Work out your own salvation with fear and trembling," but we never go on to the next verse. There's only a comma between verses 12 and 13. Verse 13 says, "For it is God who works in you both to will and to do for His good pleasure" (NKJV). I needed to invite the Lord not just to save me but to fill me and to inhabit me and to be my Lord and to baptize me in the Holy Spirit and to give me the power, not only to do His will, but to want to do it. When Shirley and I were both in our mid-30s, we received the baptism in the Holy Spirit. It changed our lives, even though it cost us continued fellowship with the church I had been raised in.

Q: Where did you find a church home?

We wound up at The Church on the Way with Pastor Jack

Hayford. It had only about 100 members then. We didn't come close to filling the building, but every service there were things that were said and done and prayed that brought us to tears and worship in a way that we never had experienced.

Every service was vital and real and a visit with God, and we couldn't help but invite friends to come. We wanted them to experience what we experienced. I've been an elder there for about 35 years now. We've watched the church grow to more than 10,000 members.

Q: **How did the Baptism continue to impact your life?**

Once I had been filled with the Spirit, I discovered I don't have to be one person when I'm with show-business people, somebody else at church, and somebody else in the business world or on the sports field or wherever. I can be the same person all the time. And I'm not going to be ashamed of the gospel, and I'm not going to be ashamed of the Lord, and I'm not going to be ashamed if they want to call me Goody-Goody or whatever they want to call me. That's OK. At least people know that I'm a Christian, and to me that's the most important designation that can be. Once that was settled in my own thinking, a lot of my decisions became easy, about where I go, who I'm with, what I do.

God has led me into some things that I would not have intellectually chosen for myself. For instance, having Ozzy Osbourne move in next door to me and eventually declare on his TV show that I am the best neighbor his family's ever had. They're lovable people. But their lifestyle — the things that seem so funny and that people actually want to hear and see from them — are certainly not a good, regular diet for us in an already polluted environment. Kids around the country will start emulating them. But, you know, when I went to visit with the Osbournes, I never heard them using all that language.

At a recent benefit for Larry King's cardiac foundation, Dana Carvey was introduced. I was way at the back of the room. Dana said, "I've got to keep it PG tonight. Pat Boone's here." Years ago, Don Rickles and I were on the *Tonight Show* together. Don started to say something to Johnny Carson, then he looked over at me and did a sort of double take and said, "I can't tell you that with Boone sitting here."

I'm not trying to intimidate anybody; they're free to do what they want. I do what I think is right. But it is a restraining influence. It has an effect on their behavior.

Q: Your latest project has given you another great opportunity to talk about God to a lot of people.

This is a real phenomenon, and it's just God. I recently put out an album called *American Glory*. It's full of patriotic songs, and it reminds people that our patriotic songs point us to God. A song I wrote for the album, "Under God," has even made it to the top-100 chart. We call these songs "patriotic," but every one of them mentions God as our Source, our Defender, our Hope and our Strength.

I asked Ollie North, a wonderful Christian guy and a retired Marine colonel, "When's the last time you heard somebody sing the Marine hymn except Marines?" He scratched his head a second and said, "I can't remember ever hearing anybody sing it except Marines." I said, "One proud non-Marine is singing your hymn in gratitude to God for you."

Q: What inspired you to put together such an album?

The inspiration for the project came to me when Michael Newdow in San Francisco stunned the nation by getting some liberal judges to side with him in his assertion that "under God" violated some separation of church and state principle. He didn't want his daughter in school to be saying "under God" in the Pledge of Allegiance sanctioned by the school. And these two judges agreed in the Ninth Circuit Court of Appeals.

I decided to fight this the only way I can, with music. And I wrote "Under God." I thought we needed a refresher course in American history. So I started with the pilgrims and then went to George Washington at Valley Forge, and then to the Constitutional Convention where Ben Franklin called for daily prayer as they were trying to draft the Constitution itself, and then to Thomas Jefferson. In the last chorus I sing, we pledge allegiance to the flag of the United States. And I do the Pledge of Allegiance at the conclusion of the record with a lot of school kids saying it with me. And that's the way the record ends — on the triumphant note, "under God, with liberty and justice for all."

Q: What kind of response have you seen?

At personal appearances there would be veterans in wheelchairs sometimes pushed by their wives and they had on their Marine or Navy caps. They would say, "I want to thank you for doing my song," and their chin would be trembling. And I'd say, "Brother, I did the song, but I want to thank you. I'm thanking you for what you've done for this country and for me and for my family."

Q: Any other thoughts?

I want to be like Jesus, who was willing to seek out people and take time with them, while never losing sight of who He is. Jesus was castigated by religious leaders and even questioned by His own disciples about fellowshiping with publicans and sinners. He was never compromising who He is, but He loved the people and He wanted them to know it. He was not embarrassed to be associated with them because He came to save them. We think we're so pure, and, like the Pharisees, don't want to have anything to do with the publican and the sinner. Yet Jesus would go right into their home and sit down and say, "What's for dinner?"

— *Ken Horn*

Bobby Bowden
How would Christ handle this?

Bobby Bowden, football coach at Florida State University in Tallahassee, had guided his Seminoles to 21 bowl appearances by 2003. The Seminoles' victory over Virginia Tech in the 2002 Gator Bowl gave Bowden his 323rd career coaching victory, tying him with Bear Bryant.

Q: **How did Christ come into your life?**

I was fortunate enough to be raised in a Christian home. As soon as I was big enough to be put in a basket, my parents carried me to church. I was raised in a Southern Baptist church.

I made a profession of faith when I was 10 or 11 years old. In the Baptist church, that means you walk down to the altar, profess your faith to the pastor, and tell him you want to be baptized and join the church. So that's what I did. I got baptized, joined the church, and began to grow in the Lord.

However, it wasn't until I was 23 that I really dedicated my life to God. By then I began to understand what grace is and what it means to be saved. I knew I had to be saved and confess my sins, but I also realized I had to do more than just be a member of the church.

Q: **In what ways do you attempt to convey a Christlike spirit to other members of one of the country's greatest college football programs?**

The best thing I can do is try to live how Christ wants me to live. He instructs us to follow His example. That's the big thing — doing things the way Jesus himself would do them. When I'm faced with a tough decision, I always try to stop and think, *Now, how would Christ handle this situation?*

Doing things the way Christ would do them sets the greatest example of all. If you try to live like Jesus wants you to and handle situations the way He would, it speaks volumes. People realize true disciples of Christ are indeed different. It's that Christlike lifestyle that sets them apart.

So I let my lifestyle minister to my players and fellow coaches.

Q: **Describe your relationship with the Fellowship of Christian Athletes.**

I have been a member of the Fellowship of Christian Athletes since 1963 — when I found out they existed.

Everywhere I have coached — Samford University, West Virginia University, and Florida State University — I have appointed a coach on my staff to handle FCA matters. We have an active FCA program here at Florida State. Many of our players are involved. We participate in outreaches and I speak at banquets occasionally.

Q: **Coaching a top-notch college football team has to be stressful.**

The thing I have to be careful about is not to do something out of desperation or excitement that I'm not supposed to do. I constantly remind myself to keep my cool with three words: Don't blow it.

Jesus faced some extreme pressure when He was on earth and He came through. We, likewise, should come through for Him.

Q: What feedback do you get from players who have accepted Christ as a result of your influence?

I've been coaching college football 42 years now. I've seen a lot of kids come and go. It's always a thrill to get a letter from an ex-player thanking me for my instruction in the ways of Christ. I've had quite a few boys write and tell me I said or did something on such-and-such a date that really ministered to them. I love to hear how I helped them do something for the glory of God.

We have had quite a few players get saved in our Fellowship of Christian Athletes program. I hear testimonies from them and I thank God.

— *James Bilton*

Bill Bright
'Not I, but Christ'

Bill Bright, founder of Campus Crusade for Christ International, authored more than 100 books and booklets and thousands of articles. He passed away on July 19, 2003, from complications related to pulmonary fibrosis. He was 81. He shared his thoughts on ministry in this 2002 interview.

Q: **You've had more than 50 years of multifaceted ministry. What is your passion right now?**

Jesus. He is my passion. From the time I awaken each morning until I go to bed at night, He is the One with whom I am in communication. And since seeking and saving the lost was His passion, that is my passion. But it is because of my love for Him that I share that passion. I try to evaluate everything I do every day in light of the Great Commission because that's why He came. People often ask me, "What is the most important thing we can pray for?" I pray that I will never leave my first love. That's the joy and burden of my heart — that I may love Jesus, know Him better, and serve Him more faithfully and fruitfully.

Q: **You mentioned the Great Commission is so very important. Why do you think so many Christians fail to witness?**

Fear and lack of knowledge. The Scripture tells us that the flesh wars against the spirit and the spirit against the flesh. Most Christians don't understand the role of the Holy Spirit. They don't realize that they cannot live the Christian life in their own strength. And they can't witness in their own strength. Jesus made very clear that the Holy Spirit would empower us to witness and to live a holy life. So there is a lack of knowledge of their role, who they are in Christ — crucified, buried, raised with Him, seated with Him in the heavenlies. We are members of the royal family. We are children of the living Creator, God. And we are to be filled with and directed by the Holy Spirit.

There are only two kingdoms in the world. We, as members of Christ's kingdom, have the privilege of invading Satan's kingdom. Colossians 1:13,14 tells us that "[God] has rescued us out of the darkness and gloom of Satan's kingdom and brought us into the kingdom of his dear Son, who bought our freedom with his blood and forgave us all our sins" *(The Living Bible)*. But the average believer is not sure of his or her salvation according to our many surveys.

The only way we can go to hell is by following the devil. Hell is made for Satan and his angels, not for us. Now if we insist on following the devil, hell is where we will go. And if we only allow Jesus to live and love through us, we follow Him in His kingdom and to our ultimate destiny in heaven. I think we need to talk more about heaven and hell.

Q: **How do you personally get direction from the Holy Spirit?**

I live according to Philippians 2:13. It is my daily reminder. "For God is at work within you, helping you want to obey him" *(The Living Bible)*. Whatever He wills you to do, He gives you power to do, the provision to do. So the first thing I do when I awake in the morning is to pray with my dear wife and then read the Scripture before I have breakfast or anything else and I acknowledge that Jesus is my Lord. In fact, 51 years ago, my wife and I signed a contract to be slaves of Jesus, He being our model. Philippians 2:7 tells us that the great Creator of the universe came to planet Earth disguised as a slave. Paul speaks of himself in Romans 1:1 as a slave.

Years ago, I was in business in Hollywood. Gold was my god. I worked day and night to make money. Then I fell in love with Jesus and went to Princeton Seminary the next year. I was spiritually illiterate. Because I was running my business all the way across the continent, God gave me an opportunity to move to Fuller Seminary when it started in 1947. I was in the first class there. I was growing. In 1948, Vonette and I were married. About two years later, we had come to the place where we realized that knowing, loving and serving Jesus were all that really mattered. We had both been very materialistic, very self-centered. Now we were falling in love with Jesus. So we signed a contract — literally wrote it out and signed it, relinquishing ourselves and all we owned to Jesus to serve Him wherever He called. I thought I would continue business. But approximately 24 hours later God spoke to me in a dramatic way and gave me the vision we call Campus Crusade for Christ. I am convinced that had there been no contract, there would have been no vision.

For these 51 years I have been a slave. I am a slave by choice. When I awake in the morning, I simply say, "Lord Jesus, walk around in my body, think with my mind, love with my heart, speak with my lips, seek and save the lost through me, do whatever You want in and through me. I'm available to do as You wish." I look back over all of these 51 years. All the miracles, awesome beyond words to describe. I've been an observer. People give me credit, but it's a Galatians 2:20 thing — not I, but Christ. The best thing you can say about Bill Bright and his wife, Vonette, is "They are slaves of Jesus."

Q: Is there hope for national revival in the United States?

In 1994, God so troubled my spirit over the decadence of our country, I fasted and prayed for 40 days for national and world revival and the fulfillment of the Great Commission. It was at that time God began to impress upon me that He was going to send a great revival. He also instructed me to call together Christian leaders to fast and pray with me. Six hundred fifty people came. Thomas Trask, Chuck Colson, Shirley Dobson and people who were heads of various denominations came and we humbled ourselves before God. It was the beginning of something magnificent. Since that time, I have been impressed to write four books on fasting and prayer. Now millions of people all over the world are fasting and praying for revival. In my opinion, there is no way to meet the conditions of 2 Chronicles 7:14 apart from fasting and prayer. Nobody is going to fast for 40 days with a big ego. Something happens. You see God's face. When you analyze it, every problem you have starts with self, ego. Fasting deals with ego more than anything else. So, yes, I'm optimistic to believe that we are going to see an awakening. Today there is harmony and love and unity among many believers where in years past it would have been impossible to work together. Each year since 1994 I have fasted and prayed for 40 days to this end.

Q: Anything else?

My plea to the body of Christ is don't allow anyone or anything to rob you of your first love. You can't maintain your first love apart from the Holy Spirit. You can't maintain your first love apart from daily reading the Scriptures, meditating on God's Word. You can't live a first-love relationship unless you obey God. So my plea is to keep your eyes on Father, Son and Holy Spirit. Know, love, trust and obey God.

We are complete in Jesus. Just think of the miracle. He lives within us — Father, Son and Holy Spirit. All the supernatural resources of deity are available to God's children. There is no limit to Him. We honor God when we think big, when we pray big, when we plan big. Not foolishly, but prayerfully. Jesus said, "This is to my Father's glory, that you bear much fruit, showing yourselves to be my disciples" (John 15:8).

— *Ken Horn*

Charles Buck
God and business

Charles Buck is the third generation in his family to operate Buck Knives. As chairman, he and his son C.J. (president and CEO) head up the company that was begun by his grandfather Hoyt Buck. Now located in El Cajon, Calif., Buck Knives has a long history of crafting some of the world's best knives ... and presenting the gospel.

Q: How did Buck Knives get started?

My grandfather had made knives in his basement for airmen during World War II, and in 1945 he moved to San Diego and talked my dad into making knives with him for a living. My dad was a bus driver at the time and didn't think he could make a living making knives. But God put the whole thing together. For example, my dad almost lost his hand in a meat grinder. If he'd lost the hand, Buck Knives wouldn't have been. He couldn't have ground the files into knives. Just as he was going into surgery the doctor said he planned to amputate, but Dad protested. People in our Assemblies of God church prayed, and he regained full use of his hand.

So they went to work together, my grandfather shaping the blades and my dad, the handles. They made five a day and sold them for $5 apiece. It was a struggle. We incorporated the business in 1961, and it began to roll. Our mark has been black handles with silver blades.

But we didn't know how to run a business, and we ran out of money. My dad had only taken a home correspondence course on accounting. In 1963 we faced a severe financial crisis. I remember Dad calling the board in and saying, "We need to pray. I don't know what the answer is, but I feel it's God's will that our business survive." We knelt down and asked God what to do, and that night when Dad went to bed he had a man's name strongly impressed on his mind. The next day he called the man, a civic leader, who said he loved the knives, and who introduced us to the bank president. He loaned us money, using our receivables as collateral. So we had immediate cash. And he recommended that we sell more equity in our business, which we did. Buck Knives grew 25 percent a year after that.

Q: Talk about your relationship with Christ.

I came to the Lord as a young man and was filled with the Spirit when I was a teenager. I was involved in our Assemblies of God church for many years. I met my wife at an Assemblies of God church across town. I've served on church boards, been a bus driver and Sunday School teacher. The Assemblies of God has been a big part of my life.

Q: You have printed a gospel message that comes with your knives.

Yes. We asked Dad if we could send a message about God with the millions of knives we send out. Dad thought it was a great idea, and it seemed like the Holy Spirit guided his hand when he wrote that message that begins by talking about the knife and segues into how God is the senior partner in our business. I've also added the text of John 3:16 because I want people to understand that you get to the Heavenly Father through Christ.

I get hundreds of letters from Christians encouraging us, pastors who read it to their congregations, and Christians in business who want to do something similar. I tell them to treat the business as if God is the senior partner. That's what we do here. I get a couple of letters from atheists every year who say we're cramming religion down their throats. I write back saying we're just so excited about Jesus Christ that we want to tell all our friends. I figure we can plant the seed, someone else can cultivate, and maybe they'll come to the Lord.

I got a letter from a lady who was going to commit suicide. She went to the hardware store to buy a pocket knife to cut her wrists with, and she was attracted to one of our knives. She took it home and read the message. When she read the last line, "If any of you are troubled or perplexed or looking for answers, may we invite you to look to Him, for God loves you," she felt joy.

"Don't ever quit putting that message in," she wrote to me.

Q: How has God blessed your business?

I pray every day that He will help us make right decisions and open doors for us. If I didn't do that, and if we didn't know the Lord, I don't really know how successful Buck Knives would be. God has enhanced our name in the marketplace, I believe because we give Him the glory. In the large cafeteria at our plant, we've always had start-up churches meet there on Sunday to generate savings to buy their own buildings. We pay all the expenses.

We've had concerns that, if we ever sold the business, probably the first thing to happen is the message about God would be taken out of our knife boxes. That's been one of the strongest reasons we've felt led not to sell, even though we get many offers. All the key positions here are held by family members. God has blessed us with good workers. Whenever we have sales meetings, I open in prayer.

Q: Would you call Buck Knives a "Great Commission" business?

Absolutely. I feel like I'm in the mission field right here. For a while we had an outside company making our pocket knives. We would send back shipments if they didn't meet Buck quality. The company decided they didn't want to throw away those knives anymore, but to grind our name off and sell them. To avoid that, I offered to buy a shipment of knives back for a dollar apiece. Three weeks later we got 60,000 knives back. I didn't know how many there were, and realized I'd made a mistake. I got on my knees and asked God to forgive me for not being a good steward and to give me an opportunity to make good.

Two weeks later I got a call from a sales representative who had just found the Lord. He told me he had given some Buck knives to a missionary couple who took them to Africa and traded them in exchange for help in building a home. I knew then what I should do. We shipped the knives to missionaries overseas who used them for barter. I've gotten letters from missionaries who said they gained great favor with elders and chieftains of local tribes because of the knives. We still send returned knives to missionaries in the field.

— *Joel Kilpatrick*

Gracia Burnham
Grace in the jungle

Gracia Burnham is the widow of Martin Burnham, who served for 17 years as a missionary pilot in the Philippines. The Burnhams were kidnapped and held as hostages in the jungle for more than a year by a radical terrorist group before Martin was killed in a rescue attempt in the summer of 2002. Burnham's book, In the Presence of My Enemies, *chronicles her ordeal.*

Q: **Do you think most Christians are prepared for the test of faith that you and Martin faced?**

God says He doesn't test you beyond what you are able to endure. I think each person's testing must be in proportion to what faith God has given them. I don't think I was able to drum up any special faith when I was going through this. I think it was all God's doing. He gave me what I needed day by day. Walking closely with Him and knowing His Word well is really going to help you when you face whatever testing comes your way.

Q: **You are candid in your book about your struggle with faith and anger with God. How did you reconcile that in the jungle?**

One of the hardest things about our captivity was that I realized what kind of person I was. I always thought I was a pretty good Christian — and then I found myself feeling hatred and covetousness and all these things I didn't want to think existed in me. But God showed me I didn't have to beat myself over the head with all that. You just acknowledge your sin, ask forgiveness and go on. If I had hit myself over the head with my sinfulness I never would have gotten out of the depression I was in out there. I learned a lot about my sinfulness, but I also learned a lot about grace.

Q: **What did you learn about God's will?**

God's will is not our will. If it all had been up to me, this wouldn't have happened. It certainly wouldn't have gone on for a year, and it most certainly wouldn't have ended with Martin's death. But God has a plan. I remember one day the kids and I were out driving and they had a CD playing. The song was "God Is God and I Am Not" by Steven Curtis Chapman. I had never heard that song before — I'd been in the jungle for a year — and that song just said it all for me. God's will is always right and always good. I feel like God's will was done in this whole thing whether I liked it or not. I'm not going to try to second-guess God's goodness or His plan.

Q: **What do you want the world to know about Martin Burnham?**

Martin was an ordinary guy who loved the Lord. I got to watch him live out his faith for a year in a horrible situation, and he was just a normal guy who let the Lord use him. I think he would laugh if he heard people say he was a hero.

Q: How are you and your children doing today?

Very well. We laugh a lot together. We talk about Martin a lot. On the whole we're doing really well. I can't really explain that. I think we've just chosen to go on and trust God.

Q: Any other thoughts?

Each person can make a difference in his or her corner of the world. You don't have to go to a foreign land; you don't have to dream for an elusive career. Right where God's put you, you can make a difference if you'll just allow Him to use you. I encourage people to go for it.

— Ashli O'Connell

Brett Butler
Faith, cancer and salvation

Brett Butler began his major league baseball career on August 20, 1981, at the age of 24. He was diagnosed with throat cancer in May 1996, but after treatment he returned to play at the end of the 1996 season. He retired in 1997 after 17 seasons on five different teams.

Q: **Describe the ordeal you went through in 1996.**

In January of 1996 I had a sore throat. The doctor gave me an antibiotic just prior to spring training, saying the condition should be gone in 7 to 10 days. Well, it never went away.

About a month into the regular season the pain was getting worse. I flew home to Atlanta. My tonsils were about the size of a plum. The lump was removed and it was cancerous. On May 20 the doctors removed 50 lymph nodes — one of them was malignant. I went through radiation.

I returned to the Dodgers on September 6.

Q: **You often mention to the media that your faith in God was vital to your swift recovery. How was your faith challenged during the rehabilitation?**

I've been a born-again Christian since 1973. I've had other miracles happen, but when you hear *cancer* you think death. Yes, my faith was challenged. First, I questioned God. We have that right as long as we allow God to take care of the situation.

One day it seemed as though God opened my eyes to remind me that He'd taken me from a 5-foot, 89-pound high school freshman and put me in the big leagues for 16 years. Then the focus shifted to my wife and kids. God revealed to me there was no way I could love my family as much as He does. "Let Me use you; trust Me," God seemed to tell me. I began to grasp that my cancer situation was bigger than I am, and I said, "Lord, use me in whatever manner You want."

Q: Tell about your salvation experience.

During my sophomore year of high school I went to a Fellowship of Christian Athletes conference in Fort Collins, Colo. As we were gathered in an auditorium, the question was asked, "If you died tonight, would you go to heaven?" I thought I was a pretty good person, but I didn't have that confidence deep down in my soul that I would go to heaven if I died. I got down on my knees and asked Christ into my life.

Q: What does Brett Butler do to let his light shine in the major league baseball community?

I'm on the board of an organization called PAO — Professional Athletes Outreach. Basically, it's Christian athletes who seek out other pro athletes, share Christ, and tell them how they can effectively minister. My wife and I have served on the board for more than 10 years.

I think it's the responsibility of professional athletes to be positive role models, not only for the kingdom of God but also for people in general. I've been involved with FCA since high school. I've ministered to youth groups and put on clinics.

I'm involved with Baseball Chapel. (Baseball Chapel is an organized ministry for baseball players that consists of chapel services on Sunday mornings.) I've been the chapel leader on my team for many years.

Q: **What advice do you have for others who are battling cancer or other life-threatening diseases?**

For those battling cancer, faced with the thought of death, I would tell them to understand that "to live is Christ and to die is gain" (Philippians 1:21). Obviously, we don't want to die. But we have to refrain from putting limits on God and understand that He would not give us a situation we cannot handle. God says, "I know the plans I have for you … plans to prosper you and not to harm you, plans to give you hope and a future" (Jeremiah 29:11). However hard it may be, we must live by this promise.

My advice is simply this: Don't limit God. He knows exactly what's going on in your life. And it's your responsibility to trust Him.

I lost my mother to cancer in August 1996. My prayer was always, "Lord, if You're going to take her, please don't let her suffer." Her doctor told me she was the only cancer patient he'd had who didn't experience pain until several days before she died. That situation can be related this way: Have the courage to say, "Lord, whatever Your purpose is for me in this situation, please fulfill that purpose." And trust God to do what's best.

— *James Bilton*

Dennis Byrd
Life after football

Dennis Byrd was a second-round draft pick of the New York Jets in 1989. Byrd's career as a National Football League defensive lineman came to an end when he broke his neck during a November 1992 game and was left paralyzed. His miraculous recovery became subject matter for a book and movie.

Q: **In the years since your miraculous recovery from paralysis what has happened in your life?**

There's been a tremendous amount of spiritual growth and maturity as a man. On the physical side, there's been a great deal of change. When I left the hospital, I was fairly anti-ambulatory. I was actually in a wheelchair. I could walk, but because of poor stamina and other things I was in a wheel-chair. But I quickly progressed to crutches and then a cane. I still use the cane at times. I had another daughter. These are the things that are so important to me: my children and my wife, our church and our relationship with God.

Q: **How long were you hospitalized and are there still aftereffects from your injury?**

I spent two and a half months in the hospital. I still have physical weakness in my body. There's something called central nerve pain that I still feel quite a bit. The thing about a spinal cord injury is that it is difficult to make a prognosis and have any hope of that prognosis staying the same because there's so much pain.

There can't be any question of the miraculous physical healing I've had. But there are still a number of physical disabilities. However, we read in the Bible that at times people were left with things to help keep them focused. Not everything is taken away as far as the physical limitations and impairments. It's my belief that many of these things remain so I won't lose focus on God, that I'll always rely on the Lord.

Q: **After your injury, you said, "I'm glad it was me and not someone else."**

I knew as a physical man and as a Christian man I would be able to handle the situation. I had the belief I wasn't alone. I was worried if it was a teammate or someone I loved very much that they weren't grounded or rooted in the same way I was. If this injury had to happen to someone, I wanted it to be me. I knew how I would react to God. I hope that doesn't minimize the injury or the severity of it or the fears I had. But through prayer, reading the Bible and people ministering to me, I was able to draw strength and realize that these problems were only temporary even if they were for the rest of my life.

Q: **Looking back to the time of your injury and recovery, what specific incidents or experiences have remained strongest in your memory?**

Whenever my teammates gathered around my bed, I had the opportunity to let them know I loved and cared for them.

The most important thing I wanted them to know was that I was a Christian and I wanted the same thing for them. I had peace and wanted them to have that same peace. I got to be a testimony and an example to those I was so close to. In a time when all of us needed help, they were struggling with why this could happen to me.

There was one time when I was struggling from the heartache of losing physical capacity. It's humiliating to be paralyzed. Nothing works. I was used to taking care of everything. I felt that was my role. Now I was completely dependent on everyone. I was just brokenhearted. My wife and brother-in-law were in my hospital room and we were reading Bible verses. It was at that point the Lord spoke to me in a clear and touching voice. I had hit a personal low. And He just said, "Be strong, My son, and you will walk again." I needed that. I knew I was going to be all right. All I had to do was be strong and trust in Him. And that is what I have to do.

I am a man, a physical man, and I want to affect my world in a physical way. If I want something changed, I try to change it with my hands or with my voice. But God says, "Listen, trust in Me, pray to Me, read My Word, and I'll change things. Let Me do it; because when I do it, it will be done right and when I tell you to move it will be in My will and not your will." When it's in His will, it will be done right.

God made me a warrior. He made me with a spirit and constitution that I think is uncommon. Even though He's blessed me with these things, I still have to submit to Him daily.

Q: **When you first suffered your paralysis, you had a legitimate concern for your wife's well-being and state of mind. What has taken place in your relationship with Angela?**

Because of changes in our lives that were so drastic, I told Angela, "I would understand if you left me." I realized what life was going to be like for her. She was going to have to take care of me as if I were another one of her children. Once again, it's the struggle of turning things over to God and letting Him handle and control things.

Angela told me, "Dennis, I love you. I will always love you regardless of what circumstance or situation you're in." So you can see how I have this appreciation for my wife. We always have these impressions of what other people think of us. Generally, the impression is wrong. I was wrong even as intimately as I knew my wife. She proved herself to me. I have a tremendous love for my wife. All I can do is thank God for that. She's a wonderful mother and an unbelievable wife.

Q: Tell us about the Dennis Byrd Foundation.

We started the work before I even left the hospital, as I was speaking to groups of children. We send letters of encouragement to people who have disabilities or injuries and are going through a traumatic time. We're trying to do some of the same things that people blessed us with while we were in a similar situation.

I have a football camp in Arizona. This coming summer will be the fourth year we've had it. We have hundreds of children come from the Indian reservation. It's really a leadership camp. We teach them about character, values, integrity and leadership — things they're going to need as a football player, as an athlete. But the message we're giving them is something they can take to school, into their personal relationships, and as they grow into husbands, fathers, businessmen.

We do all kinds of events and speaking engagements. We're sort of a full-service, nonprofit organization. But we only have one paid employee, Betty Hales, my mother-in-law. My time and my wife's time are volunteered.

It's amazing how good things come out of tragedy. I think that so much of it has to do with the way you look at life and your circumstances. I've looked at my cup being half full. It's hard sometimes to get people who are bitter or brokenhearted to buy into that. I am a firm believer in the fact we allow every circumstance and situation to affect us. They make us grow, or they bring us down. In the end, they either strengthen us or they break us.

Q: What were the circumstances surrounding your decision to follow the Lord Jesus Christ?

I gave my life to the Lord when I was 13 or 14 at a youth camp in the mountains of California. I was raised in church and always had a great belief in Jesus. But there comes that time when you have to make a decision for yourself. You have to really think, "OK, here's the story. Am I believing now between good and evil and the fact that this Man, Jesus Christ, is literally God, the Son of God, who came to this earth to die on the cross and shed His blood for me? If I accept that, I am forgiven of all my sins and have eternal life." I had to finally make a decision: "Do I believe in this? Yes I do. I accept Jesus as my Savior."

My mother and father, Nancy and Dan Byrd of Baton Rouge, La., had done children's ministry for a number of years. They had puppets and were great storytellers. We traveled from church to church. I had a ton of involvement. That's where I'm sure I have this tremendous love for kids. I do all these things focusing primarily on children. I have memories of things and lessons my parents taught me as a child or as a young man that affect me today. Some of them couldn't have taken more than five minutes. But they've completely changed my life. So I do that with my children. I take the time to be observant and share little things with them.

Q: How much have you missed being able to play pro football?

Oh, a bunch. I have a tremendous competitive drive. And I miss playing. That was a neat outlet for me. Football was fun.

Q: **Any closing thoughts?**

There'll be somebody out there who needs the verse that meant so much to me in the hospital: "For I reckon that the sufferings of this present time are not worthy to be compared with the glory which shall be revealed in us" (Romans 8:18, KJV). Whenever we're going through such difficult heartbreaking circumstances or situations, we don't realize if we persevere and trust in the Lord, He's going to take those trials away from us. God has made that verse happen in my life. I just trusted and believed in Him. And I have to every day.

— *Ron Kopczick*

Bob Carlisle
Songwriter and family man

Bob Carlisle, a Christian musician, wrote and recorded the hit song "Butterfly Kisses" in 1997 for his daughter Brooke. The song went on to receive dozens of awards, including a Grammy, and topped the music charts for seven weeks.

Q: **You have been a Christian artist for a long time. What does it mean to have a number one hit — "Butterfly Kisses" — on the secular charts?**

It serves to remind me there are an awful lot of good people in the world who are starving for some content in pop music about things that are good and right.

One of the greatest things we can do as Christians is affect our culture. That's what Jesus wants us to do.

Q: How do you maintain your values?

I've been married for 20 years. I've got an 18-year-old daughter and an 11-year-old son. My life doesn't revolve around the music business; my life revolves around my relationship with Jesus and my relationship with my family.

Q: In what ways is it a challenge for your family to deal with the hype of the music industry?

We live on our terms. I did not pursue an offer to sing the national anthem at last year's World Series because I had a week off and didn't want to compromise that chance to spend time with my family.

Q: How do you keep grounded spiritually?

Having a wonderful pastor. My manager is also my dear friend. We keep each other accountable. He's always good at getting me to church and making sure we keep our eyes on the Cross.

The one thing I have learned, especially this year, is that if God wants to do something, He can do it. For an overweight, 41-year-old father of two to be competing with the Spice Girls at the top of the pop charts, you can't help but see God's finger in the mix.

Q: Why do you think the public has responded so favorably to "Butterfly Kisses"?

I would like to think the response is because it reinforces something they already know to be true. Unfortunately, there are children who are longing for something they never had, and it breaks my heart. But it's a starting point. If someone can create a fire in someone to get on the phone or send a letter to that dad they haven't spoken to in a couple of years, that's God.

Q: What long-term impact will "Butterfly Kisses" have on your career?

I'll be singing it until the day I die. For a singer or songwriter to have created something that people have taken to heart — it is just amazing. It's a song that I'll always be requested to sing. It's a very heartwarming song and it's a song that I don't mind singing a lot.

Q: Why is surrender so difficult in our lives?

The hardest place to surrender is when you are struggling to fit into everybody else's mold. I feel sorry for young artists today who are trying to jump through hoops and become a certain thing.

It's not hard to be a Christian. There isn't anything I can blame if I lack a relationship with the Lord.

— *Amber Weigand-Buckley*

Cris Carter
Playing on God's team

*Former Minnesota Vikings wide receiver **Cris Carter** was famous for making one-handed catches and acrobatic sideline receptions. In the 2000 season, he became only the second player in NFL history to catch more than 1,000 passes, securing his place in the Pro Football Hall of Fame. But he will be remembered for more than his game. Fans will remember the athlete whose career and life were transformed after he accepted Christ, and the boldness with which he shared his testimony. And they will remember how after each touchdown catch, he took a knee and pointed skyward to his Heavenly Father.*

Q: **The story of your release by Buddy Ryan and the Philadelphia Eagles has been called the wake-up call of your career. Is that what caused you to look to Christ?**

It wasn't immediately after that. I realized there were aspects of my life that I wanted to change; but, as far as inviting Christ into my life, it still took several more years after that.

Q: **What eventually drew you to Him?**

My wife and I consciously decided that we knew there was a better life than what we were living. We knew that Christ was the way. It was just a matter of submitting to His will instead of doing what we wanted to do.

The hardest thing for me was realizing that, even though I was a great success, I was really nothing without God. I never really had joy in my life. I had temporary happiness, but I was never really satisfied. My only satisfaction has come through a relationship with God, and it was the best decision I've ever made. After walking with God for seven years, I don't know how I ever made it without Him. I really don't.

Q: **You're among the most visible and vocal athletes in sports when it comes to sharing your faith in Christ. Why?**

Every man casts his shadow. For me, my shadow is very big given my professional life and the recognition I have received. Young people and adults alike look up to me. So it's a tremendous opportunity to share and to show people the love of God — not only professionally what has driven me to have success, but also spiritually what guides me on a day-to-day basis.

Q: **You are viewed as a leader in the locker room. Talk about the influence you can have on your teammates from a spiritual perspective.**

The biggest role I have to play is day-to-day. How I respond to adversity. How I love my brothers. Can I be unselfish? Can I accept people, whatever their condition? Am I understanding? Am I a good listener? Those are the things that drive me.

Q: At times your actions as a leader have been criticized. What are your thoughts and feelings on dealing with the media?

Given what we're up against spiritually, I realize that the media is going to do certain things to try to discourage me and try to take things away from my testimony. God gave me great compassion. But people want to use my Christian faith to persecute me — as if I shouldn't have fire, or shouldn't challenge my teammates, or shouldn't want to win as much as I do. But they're just using it as an excuse to be critical of me. It doesn't bother me, and I realize that it's part of the territory.

Q: What has made you such a great receiver?

It's really working hard and trying to perfect the receiver position as far as technique, running good routes, being competitive daily, understanding the game, studying the game plan, studying the film and being a student of the game. Making the unbelievable catch is something that I practice and really strive for.

Q: Where do you think God may be leading you when your playing days are over?

I'll be involved in worldwide evangelism, at least part-time. Sharing the gospel, sharing my story, sharing my life with people who are really hurting. My wife and I might also counsel youth and young married couples about how Christ led us out of a very average relationship into a great relationship.

Q: Many reading this interview may be confronted with the gospel for the first time. Maybe they're on the fence and they aren't quite ready to make a decision for Christ. What would you say to them?

You're either in, or you're not. There is no in-between. You either love Him and want to submit to Him, or you're going to do your own thing. The one thing I always try to convey to people is, "You're either working for God or you're working for the enemy." And you have to realize that the sooner you get on God's team the sooner you're going to have victory in your life.

— *Paul Cossentine*

Dr. David Yonggi Cho
The work of the Holy Spirit

Dr. David Yonggi Cho is pastor of the Yoido Full Gospel Church in Seoul, South Korea. The world's largest church, it serves more than 800,000 members. He is also founder, president and chairman of the board of directors for Church Growth International and past chairman of the World Assemblies of God Fellowship.

Q: What is the importance of the Holy Spirit in the believer's life?

Without the influence of the Holy Spirit, no one can believe in the Lord. The Holy Spirit is the heaven-sent Helper for our Christian life. Without His help, we can't survive in this world of evil. This is the age of the Holy Spirit. God the Father and Jesus the Son manifest to us through the Holy Spirit.

Q: What advice would you give someone who is seeking the baptism in the Holy Spirit? What steps should they take?

To receive the baptism in the Holy Spirit:
1) One should thoroughly confess sins.
2) One should completely surrender to our Lord Jesus.
3) One should fervently desire the fullness of the Holy Spirit.
4) One should persistently pray for the fullness of the Holy Spirit.

Q: Do the gifts of the Spirit continue to be an important part of what God is doing in Korea? Do you still see miracles frequently?

We are seeing miracles abundantly here in Korea. Where the Holy Spirit is present, the gifts must be manifest, and Christians have to expect the manifestation of the gifts. Divine healing is an integral part of the good news. This message has to be preached. Faith comes by hearing. The lack of preaching and teaching on this cause the disappearance of divine healing.

Q: Why do you think miracles occur in some places and not in others?

Miracles occur when you desire and expect and believe. When people stop reading the Bible and stop accepting God's promises, the Holy Spirit does not perform miracles.

Q: Some people are confused about how to pray for healing. How would you suggest they pray?

Healing is included in the redemption of our Lord. Healing is given through grace by faith, so one should know the healing promises and believe, and persistently pray and claim.

Q: As you travel the world in ministry, are you seeing churches in revival?

Generally, I see churches in revival in Africa, Asia, and in South America. Churches are dying in Europe. The

Pentecostal churches are growing and are very healthy. Any church where the Holy Spirit is welcome, the church is coming alive.

Q: What has the Lord laid upon your heart at this time in your ministry?

Awakening the body of Christ for the soon coming of our Lord Jesus Christ.

Q: What are your current goals and dreams?

In two years, I should resign when I become 70 years old. But presently my goal is planting 500 to 1,000 new churches in Korea and to evangelize North Korea and China.

Q: Anything else you would like to share with our American readers?

The American church has always been a source of inspiration and our pride. I pray that God may revive the American church to renew the strength and leadership for world Christendom.

— *Ken Horn*

Bobby Clampett
Sharing Jesus on the links

Bobby Clampett was on the PGA Tour from 1980 to 1995, and is now a course reporter with CBS Sports. His best finish came in 1982 when he won the Southern Open in Columbus, Ga. As a professional golfer, Clampett founded Players Outreach Ministries. He and his family live in North Carolina.

Q: **How did you come to faith in Christ?**

People come to Christ in different ways. For some it's a slow process. There were key players God put in my path.

The most significant impact occurred when I met my wife. She had been brought up in the church and made a commitment to Christ when she was 17. We met my third year of the PGA. I was still hanging on to preconceived church beliefs that I had picked up in the Christian Science church and the Mormon church. We enjoyed talking about spiritual issues, and both of us were seekers of truth.

There were many questions that couldn't be answered by the Christian Scientists or Mormons. I knew there was objective truth out there, but I didn't want to join a church and commit intellectual suicide. My wife played a big part in the process, and so did other Christians on the tour. I was moving toward the belief that the Bible is the inspired Word of God and that Jesus is who He claimed to be. I began to realize I had never made a decision to trust Him for my salvation and allow Him to change me and be at the forefront of my life. I did that in July 1984. I was very self-centered before then.

God has changed me. It was the one decision that has most profoundly impacted my life.

Q: You exude a Christlike attitude on the golf course.

Jesus said that He came to bring abundant life (John 10:10). I try to display that abundance on the golf course. It comes as a direct result of our obedience to Him when He fills us with the joy that brings abundance.

Q: How do you keep balance in your life with all the touring, family activities and Christian responsibilities?

There are ongoing challenges — especially with me traveling and being separated from my family. I travel less than I used to, but it comes down to making intentional, Christ-honoring choices. That's where Christian character comes in.

Q: The Christian witness within the PGA has been growing. What is the spiritual climate like in the PGA? Do you see spiritual renewal taking place?

No question about it. The PGA Tour Bible study began in 1966 with five players. The study has grown tremendously. There are 250 or so players on the tour, and 70 have made a public confession of Christ.

It's just amazing to watch the power of God at work in the lives of people. I'm excited to see people deepen their walk with God and seek truth. We're blessed on the PGA Tour with people who are diligently seeking God. They are not seeking some spiritual thing to hold on to; they're looking for truth. Players are seeking answers to life's deeper questions. I think specifically in my age group there seems to be a real awakening. I believe we are in a time of spiritual awakening.

— *Don Spradling*

Admiral
Vern E. Clark
Serving Christ and country

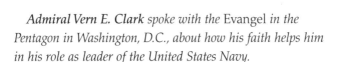

Admiral Vern E. Clark spoke with the Evangel *in the Pentagon in Washington, D.C., about how his faith helps him in his role as leader of the United States Navy.*

Q: **You grew up in an Assemblies of God preacher's home.**

Yes, I was taught at an early age what it means to commit your life to Christ. The key thing about my walk is that my mom and dad spent a lot of time talking about God's call for me. That led me to Evangel University. This position is where the Lord has placed me now. I have spent my life going through doors that He has opened.

Q: **What unique challenges do you face in a position of this magnitude?**

Every Christian has the challenge of being faithful to his or her commitment — to maintain a life that feeds the spiritual man. Admiral Jay Johnson, my predecessor, was once asked, "What are you looking for in people in your officers corps?"

He said he wanted people who are trustworthy; people with integrity and moral values; people whose yes means yes and whose no means no.

So these strengths in a Christian's walk are needed of anyone who would succeed in any career. I am in a profession where integrity is vitally important. When you are in a situation where lives are on the line, you had better be a person of integrity.

There are times that I feel inadequate to the task. Throughout my career, my faith has sustained me through some tough situations.

Q: Could you tell us about some difficult experiences?

I have commanded three ships, two squadrons of destroyers, a carrier battle group and then a fleet. The times when you feel it most are when things are riding on your decisions and the stakes are high. I commanded a destroyer in a hurricane. In the Mediterranean, we were face-to-face, at very short range, with the ships of the then Soviet Union — tense situations. I have characterized my life as a series of short prayers. When those moments come that's the time the Lord says He will be with us.

Q: What do you do to maintain your devotional life?

My wife, Connie, gets up with me and we have devotions and pray. We ask God to help us to find where He is moving and that we would be an effective part of it. I make it a point every day to sit down in the middle of this chaos and again commit a few minutes to read and pray. Once a week I have a friend who comes and spends 30 minutes with me and we talk about spiritual things. Our wonderful church also ministers to us.

Q: What would you say to Christians about how to pray for and support the military?

Our people are spread all over the face of the globe and they need our prayers. There's more activity and danger than there has ever been. The commitment of these young people is really incredible. We need to keep focused not on the political pieces, but to pray for the spiritual health of our servicemen and women. When that's in line, the other things are going to be fine.

— *Ken Horn*

Nicky Cruz
Working to save children

Nicky Cruz became known through his autobiography, Run Baby Run, *which chronicled his journey from New York City gang involvement to his life-changing encounter with Jesus Christ under the ministry of David Wilkerson. More than 40 years after his salvation experience, Cruz is an Assemblies of God minister who leads TRUCE Invasions (To Reach Urban Children Everywhere), a growing part of Nicky Cruz Outreach.*

Q: **What are you seeing at your TRUCE Invasions?**

What impresses me is the pain, and the hurt, and the suffering, and the guilt that people are keeping in this generation. This is not just an inner-city problem; this is a people problem, from all walks of life, all kinds of races and creeds. Parents and good-looking kids, as well as guys with tattoos, all come to the altars, all crying like little babies. A lot of parents in the church have kids involved with drugs, gangs and stealing. Christian parents are going through heavy situations.

Of course, the youth are still fascinated with my past. I don't know why, because I am no longer that young kid. But I think they can see my heart. They sense that I feel today the way that they think. It is amazing that I can really still break through and reach them.

Q: **How have gangs changed since your involvement with the Mau-Maus in the 1950s?**

With today's kids, if you look bad at them they say, "You disrespected me, I'm going to blow your head off." The senseless violence has increased so much and the hearts of the young people have been torn apart and been replaced with the hardest heart that I have ever seen.

Q: **In *Run Baby Run*, you described yourself as "an animal without conscience, morals, reason, or any sense of right and wrong." Yet you still say gangs had standards that were different?**

Absolutely. I was an animal in a territory where the strongest survives. Survival was the name of the game. And I'll tell you one thing to go deeper into that statement. When I was locked up in jail is when I began to deal with my two natures. In the Bible, Paul really put it so beautifully. In Romans 7 he described how even the Christian will struggle with the two natures. When you want to do good, you do wrong. You are being trapped by a nature that wants to pull you down.

When I was in jail, sometimes at 3 or 4 in the morning I could not sleep. The silence, the quietness, was so strong that you could hear the breath of the other people. And there I was smoking a cigarette. Not only was I smoking a cigarette … I was smoking my mind. I began to philosophize with myself: If I am a human being, why am I acting like an animal? If I am an animal, what am I doing trapped inside of a human being? Where is freedom? Where can I be free from this? There I was, for the first time, in touch with my feelings.

Q: **Any other thoughts?**

People like myself have come out of terrible backgrounds. Many have started and then lost their hearts. I never have lost my heart for the things that I believe, for the resurrection that I believe in Jesus Christ. I am thankful anytime someone who has been in trouble in gangs can look at me and say, "If Nicky Cruz made it, then I can make it too!" For 40 years I have been walking the same path. The only thing that is left for me is to embrace my Lord face to face and to kiss His feet and say, "Thank You for saving me when I was lost."

— *Scott Harrup*

Jim Cymbala
Building a church on prayer

Jim Cymbala has been pastor of the interdenominational Brooklyn Tabernacle in New York City for 33 years. During that time, the church has grown from 20 members to nearly 10,000. Cymbala lives in New York City with his wife, Carol, who directs the Brooklyn Tabernacle Choir.

Q: How do you build a church on prayer?

By praying. You find how, in your local situation, you can lead people in prayer. We began a prayer meeting, which has become the focal point of our church week. Standing-room-only audiences — 1,500 to 2,000 people crushed into the building to pray. But even during our four Sunday services we have altar services which are nothing more than mini prayer meetings — waiting on God, talking about prayer, looking at the promises concerning it and reminding ourselves that the Church was born in a prayer meeting, not a preaching session.

Q: You allow a lot of time in your Sunday services for the Holy Spirit to lead. How does He lead?

Differently every meeting. Because of the problems people bring into the meeting and because God is not an instant God, you have to take time and wait. Our meetings are two or more hours long. We don't have meetings packed on top of each other so if we call people forward to pray — a mother whose son is on crack, a guy who has tested positive for HIV, someone who wants to be set free from bondage — we don't say, "Here's your lecture, now move out so the other group can come in."

Some churches have made the sermon the centerpiece instead of the Throne of Grace.

Q: What message would you give to smaller churches?

We started with a handful of people, so I can relate. But the idea of model churches is negative because it takes people away from praying and finding what God wants them to do. The key is to get a group of core people who are in love with each other and the Lord, and get them praying. If people who are united in spirit love one another and God, and begin to pray, then if something wonderful doesn't happen we'd have to throw the Bible away.

As Charles Finney taught, every church is potentially a dynamo if the right connections are made. If there's gossip, if it's prayerless, if you don't want people of other colors, then all bets are off. But if we go through the process, are broken and pray, something wonderful has to happen. The Bible says to call upon Him and He'll answer us.

The real work of God is brokenness. When you really meet God, you are made broken and low. The deepest worship I've seen is when people break inside and say, "Lord, I am totally available to You. I'll go anywhere." Only the Spirit brings brokenness. As we wait on the Lord, we try to depend more on the Holy Spirit for things only He can produce.

Q: What are the fruits of a healthy church?

Salvations are a key fruit. That's the last thing Jesus said to do. He didn't say worship or study. He said, "Be filled with power and witness." A meeting is successful when you go home talking about Jesus. If you're talking about the church, or how clever the pastor was, you're not hitting the mark. Damage has to be done to our self-lives and we have to get more in love with Him to know we've really met the Lord.

When the Holy Spirit comes, you see yourself and God in a way no teaching can give you. It's revelation. Like we tell people here, "Don't tell people about Brooklyn Tabernacle; tell them about Jesus." What is the Tabernacle? It's another local church. My wife and I have a saying that when the tears stop and when there's not that gentle breaking in choir practices and the prayer meeting, then we're in trouble even if we have 20,000 people in our church.

Like Charles Spurgeon said, "God keeps His choicest wines in the lowest part of the cellar." You can't go too low. God's main task is to keep us humble.

— *Joel Kilpatrick*

Jo Ann Davis
The power of prayer

Jo Ann Davis serves Virginia's 1st Congressional District in the U.S. House of Representatives.

Q: What is the atmosphere and what are the challenges as a believer involved in government?

I'm not a politician first; I'm a Christian who happens to be in politics. I feel very strongly that this is the path that God led me on. I see a lot of ways in Congress, in Washington, in which God is working. I think now more than ever we have a godly man in the White House and we have Christians in the House and Senate. I believe God is trying to move and it's time now that we pray and humble ourselves.

Q: How would you recommend Christians pray for government and for the political climate in the nation?

I would pray that the leaders in government would have godly wisdom, that they would listen to the Lord and that they would be bold, step out and not worry about being politically correct. Pray that God's Spirit would descend upon Washington and upon each and every member of Congress. I ask people to pray that I would not only have wisdom but that I would be open in my spirit to hear from God, and that I would be obedient to the Lord.

Q: What are the issues that Christians should be concerned about?

Issues that impact the family are the ones that concern me the most — the homosexual agenda, the need for pro-life legislation, for example. Families are the basis of our nation.

Q: During the continuing conflict overseas, how should we be praying and supporting our troops and our leaders?

I serve on the House Armed Services Committee and International Relations Committee and I have visited our men and women in the military over in Afghanistan. We need to pray for their safety, that God will bring them back home to their families.

Q: How did you come to know Christ?

I got saved when I was 25 in 1981. My husband's sister led me to the Lord when his mother died.

Q: Describe your journey into politics.

I spent months asking God to use me. Eventually, I got my real estate license and opened a real estate company. One of my real estate agents in 1997 asked me to consider running for the state legislature against a 15-year incumbent. I was not political in any way, shape or form. I voted every year for pro-life candidates, but I didn't know anything else about them. And then my friend said those fateful words: "Would you pray about it?" So I prayed. I started to feel led by the Lord to run. I asked my husband, knowing that if he said no, I wouldn't do it. And he said, "I knew three years ago that you would do something like this." I ran for the state legislature in 1997, and started serving in 1998. I served three years and then the congressman in my district announced his retirement. I knew that I was supposed to run for Congress. I did, against all odds. Even the governor endorsed another candidate, but I knew that the Lord had told me I was going to Congress. So we ran even though we didn't have any money. We won. Here we are.

Q: Any other thoughts?

Just continue praying. There are so many of us in government who feel those prayers and we know the prayers are what keep us going. Without prayer, I couldn't be here.

— Ken Horn

Dr. Richard Dobbins
Understanding suffering

Dr. Richard Dobbins is a Christian psychologist and minister. After 26 years of pastoral experience, Dr. Dobbins launched EMERGE Ministries, a Christian mental health center in Akron, Ohio. Dobbins spoke about the impact of 9/11 on America and strategies people can use to deal with life's sorrows.

Q: **How have you observed Americans collectively responding to the pain of 9/11?**

Initially, we were in a state of shock all over the country. Our collective reaction to 9/11 leaves Americans still sensitive and in great pain. The ongoing threat of terrorism has added another level of anxiety that imposes on the whole nation many of the symptoms of post-traumatic stress disorder. That is, any time we hear something on the news that relates to terrorism the same kind of feelings we felt on 9/11 resurface. This does not begin to tap the feelings of those who lost loved ones in the tragedy. They will need at least another two to three years before recovery, and even then the scars will be very painful for a long, long time.

Q: How can followers of Jesus Christ find peace in the midst of such tragedy?

The believer looks for peace from within, not from without. God's kingdom is a kingdom of "righteousness, peace and joy in the Holy Spirit" (Romans 14:17). This is not the first time in the history of the church that believers have had to find peace or joy outside their social setting. Paul and Silas in the Philippian jail, after they had been beaten, sang praises to God at midnight. We have to rise above the level of our society and find our peace and our joy in our relationship with God. God, who enabled the martyrs to sing in the face of death, will give us peace and joy with our current state of national anxiety.

Q: What are some day-to-day coping measures we can use against life's more common disappointments?

Disappointments vary in frequency and intensity. Often, we set ourselves up for disappointment because our expectations of life and our expectations of others are unrealistically high. I think many Christians mistakenly believe that there is some way in which they can lead a protected life. Jesus taught that storms would come to everybody's home (Matthew 7:24-27). So Christians who believe that no members of their family will ever get cancer or be killed in plane crashes or automobile wrecks if they go to church every Sunday and pay their tithes and have devotions every day, are setting themselves up for big disappointments by such unrealistic expectations.

One of the ultimate disappointments is based on the fact that people don't really understand the eternal nature of our life. While we miss a relationship and we mourn the loss of a loved one, if we know Jesus we are already eternal. What we're really mourning is a 10- or 15-year loss of our loved one here, maybe longer. But the one who leaves us, if he or she is in the Lord, is not dead. And you can't shorten anything that's eternal.

For the believer, to be absent from the body is to be present with the Lord (2 Corinthians 5:8).

Q: **How can God bring blessing into our lives when we face suffering?**

First, we need to see our times of suffering as not often initiated by God. Once in a while, because of foolish decisions we make, He allows us to suffer the consequences of those decisions. But most of the time, pain comes to us from other sources than God.

Priscilla and I had a wisteria plant in our garden and it wasn't bearing many blossoms. Someone told us we needed to assault the tree. So we took a shovel and we dug the blade of the shovel into the bark of the tree several times. This last year it was just loaded with blossoms. Pain is like that. It makes you bitter or better. It kills you or it motivates your growth. When God sends pain into our lives, the intention is not to kill us. It's to motivate our growth.

Q: **What does suffering contribute to our ability to comfort others?**

I've told couples who are going through really painful times that God is preparing them to be sources of comfort to people who would find others' words hollow. Now that this person has walked in their shoes and felt their pain they are in a position to tell others how God will get them from where they are to the other side of suffering.

Q: **What is the greatest personal tragedy you have faced, and how did God pull you through it?**

My first wife, Dolores, and I faced a good many tragedies: a daughter with polio; a daughter born with a congenital heart problem that had to be corrected by surgery; I had rheumatoid arthritis as a young man and couldn't put on my own coat or drive a car. But the greatest personal tragedy was the loss of my wife. I saw her battle courageously and finally succumb to a three-year struggle with cancer. As we walked through that time together, both of us had a sense that we were surrounded by the prayers of God's people. I think sometimes people feed their fears by anticipating whether or not grace will be there when they need it. There is no way for anyone to know how they will have grace at a time of crisis. But God has always been there for all of His children. Dolores and I found that to be true. We had times — particularly when we knew that she was not going to win her struggle unless there was some miracle — when we talked about my life continuing here on earth, and her life in the presence of the Lord. Many times the comfort that God can bring to people when going through tragedy is sidetracked or hindered because they feel like it would hurt too much to talk about it. But if you can define the area of pain and you can articulate it, you can modify it. God can pour grace into you.

The worst thing you can do is to be silent — silent with God, silent with others who are going through it with you, and silent even in your own thought life. You need to embrace whatever you're going through. I had to do my grief work. It was six months before I even felt single. It was almost 18 months before I thought about bringing somebody else into my life. God gives you grace day by day.

Q: **When a person has weathered a crisis, what can be done to reinvest life with joy?**

You have to put closure to the crisis. Each of us puts closure on things in different ways, but I think many times talking to God through journals helps us to put closure on events. Ritualistic behaviors that are meaningful to us can serve that purpose. For example, I made up my mind that at Dolores' graveside I would take my wedding ring off and give it to my son as a memory of our marriage. I had the stones from her engagement and wedding rings made into jewelry for our two daughters. I've talked to people whose loved one had been dead for a year or two and their room was still kept just the way they left it. In some instances parents still set a place at the table for the child. This is not healthy grief.

However, ritualistic and symbolic behaviors that are meaningful to us can serve to process the grief. When I was in town I went to my wife's grave almost every day for one year. Confronting the realities of your life and refusing to deny the pain will eventually bring healing to you. It's like a wound in your body — the deeper the wound, the longer it takes to heal and it heals from inside out.

— Scott Harrup

Tony Hall
Feeding the hungry, one person at a time

*Nominated three times for the Nobel Peace Prize, Ambassador **Tony P. Hall** is chief of the U.S. Mission to the U.N. Agencies in Rome — The World Food Program (WFP), the Food and Agriculture Organization (FAO) and the International Fund for Agricultural Development (IFAD). Prior to entering the diplomatic corps, he was a member of the U.S. House of Representatives for almost 24 years. Hall, a follower of Jesus Christ, has made the needs of the impoverished and hungry his priority. He spoke with the Evangel in 2001 when he was still a congressman.*

Q: When did you become a believer in Jesus Christ?

About 21 years ago, and I had been in Congress about a year.

Q: What were the circumstances?

About one to two years before that, I had heard Charles Colson talk at a prayer breakfast in Dayton, Ohio. I was a state senator at the time and went because it would be a good place to be seen. I was very surprised by what he said. There was great sincerity there. About a year later I was elected to Congress. For a year I would get up every Sunday morning and go to a different church. My wife thought something was wrong with this. "What are you doing?" she'd ask. "I'm kind of searching for God but I don't know where to go," I'd say. A young freshman congressman befriended me and helped lead me to the Lord.

Q: What birthed your passion to help the poor?

It probably started in the Peace Corps. I was in Thailand for two years in the late '60s. When you're in the Peace Corps you have to live pretty much like the people do. You begin to get the feel of what these people go through on a daily basis. As a result of that experience, when I came to Congress I was drawn to the issue of poverty. At first, I didn't have the slightest idea what to do about it. Then I became a believer. Bill Bright of Campus Crusade for Christ, a good friend, mentored me for about three years. He said to me one day, "Do you think it's time you start to bring God into the workplace?" I agreed, but didn't know how. I was uneasy in those days with people who spoke about God, especially elected officials. I felt many used it for all the wrong reasons. But as I began to read the Scriptures they started to come alive in me. There are at least a couple thousand verses that deal with the poor. In 1989, after the death of Congressman Mickey Leland, I took over as chairman of the Select Committee on Hunger. We passed lots of budgets that year: food aid, child survival activities, immunizing children, development of systems — and paved the way for laws today.

Q: You encountered some challenges.

Yes. Some in Congress felt that, at a time of high deficits, they needed to start paring back, which was great in principle. But some actions were only symbolic. The first thing they did was cut the Hunger Committee. I said this was crazy; my budget was only $600,000. I was mad. So I felt I should fast. I went on a water-only fast for 22 days.

Q: Did you ever think your political career might be over?

My staff thought this was the end of my career. But I was going to fast until something major happened. A whole lot started to happen. Students at thousands of high schools around the country started to fast with me, and at a couple of hundred universities. Newspapers began to take notice. A nonprofit agency called The Congressional Hunger Center was formed. They have a national conference on hunger based around the fast. Billions of dollars over the years have been raised to fight hunger. It was a fast unto the Lord to break the chains of injustice. I was so amazed by it.

Q: Would you ever do it again?

I'd like to do it again. I've fasted on a couple of occasions but not for that length of time. Fasting has to be about the Lord first.

Q: Some people realize there are hunger problems around the world, but don't recognize the problem in the United States. Talk about hunger here and abroad.

For somewhere between 22 and 25 million people in America, hunger is a way of life. They're not starving to death, like in North Korea, but they are hungry. A lot of these people are children and people on fixed incomes like senior citizens and the working poor. By the time they pay their utility costs, rent and gasoline, they are out of money with three or four days left in the month. They end up going to food banks and soup kitchens. These are, for the most part, innocent, hardworking people. They are not on welfare. They don't qualify for government assistance or many other benefits.

Q: **What about around the world?**

An estimated 900 million people are severely malnourished. Some 25,000–35,000 people die every day from hunger in the world. The worst places are North Korea, Sudan, Sierra Leone, Afghanistan and parts of the Congo. Across Africa drought and civil war are causing hunger. In North Korea, people are surviving on maybe 300 grams of food a day, and many are eating substitute food such as bark, leaves or grass. They grind it up and make noodles out of it. There is no nutrition in it; you can't digest it. I've been there six times and the malnutrition is tragic; even among the soldiers, growth is stunted.

Q: **The world hunger problem is so large, what would you say to the average person who really wants to make a difference?**

I'd say the same things that Mother Teresa said to me. Do the things in front of you. The first time I met her in Calcutta, I asked her the same question, where do you start? In Calcutta, hundreds of thousands live on the street. She started 50–60 years ago going to the person on the street she saw first, picking him up, cleaning him off and taking him home. That was the start. Her point was that if everyone would do what was in front of them, we'd probably solve about 75 percent of our problems. You don't have to go to Calcutta; feed the people around you who you know. If the churches did what they should do, there would not be so many problems for the poor, who ought to be the top priority of believers.

Q: **Elaborate on that.**

There is this problem of a church at every corner with its own constituents. They don't share resources and they don't accomplish as much as they could. There are great exceptions. I have a lot of churches in my district that are doing very well and working hard, and I have lots of churches that are poor and can't do much. But for many churches, there is so much more they could do.

Q: **When you travel overseas one of your practices is to invite someone to come with you and pray. Tell us about that.**

I take very difficult trips to places where I see a lot of people who are hurting, a lot of children who are dying. I meet with some leaders who are scoundrels. I have found over the years that if I go with people who are believers, or at least one good friend who can pray with me at night, there is a certain strength and power that God brings. In 1 Thessalonians 1:2, Paul talks about always praying for the Thessalonians. In verse 5, he says three things happen: Believers go with power, the Holy Spirit and with true conviction. For the past two years, even when I go on official trips, I take a believer with me. We are in situations where we're well over our heads. The people we meet are more shrewd than we are; they know the local situation better than we do. They try to manipulate the process, and a lot of times they are killers.

Q: **If believers don't pick up the ball and attempt to feed the hungry, what's the future?**

We'll stay right where we are. The government will help, but we'll still have great poverty and the problems that go with poverty.

Q: **Anything else?**

Americans are basically good and decent people who give when they know about a problem. We've certainly seen that in our country's response to the September 11 attacks on the U.S. I don't think Americans know about the hungry in America. You don't see it; you have to hunt for it. You have to talk to senior citizens to discover they're making $800 a month on Social Security but their medical bills are $750 a month. You have to talk to the working poor to discover they're making maybe $6 or $7 an hour and have a couple kids. These people are shy and embarrassed. They don't want to be on welfare. If Americans ever found out about this, I think they would change. They need to see the need around them and around the world and recognize that whatever role they can play as individuals is vital.

— *Hal Donaldson*

Dallas Holm
Faith and prayer in life's toughest times

During some 40 years of ministry as a Christian musician,
Dallas Holm *has recorded 34 successful projects and given
more than 3,000 concerts. Throughout his ministry, he has
never lost sight of his family's central role in his life. Dallas
and Linda Holm have been married 35 years and have two
grown children, Jennifer and Jeffrey. Dallas spoke about one
of the greatest challenges he and his wife have faced.*

Q: **You and Linda began a very difficult journey of
faith together in 1987.**

We discovered Linda had cancer the first time in 1987. It
was already a time of transition. Our band, Dallas Holm and
Praise, which we had had for 11 years, played its last concert
on the Fourth of July 1987 at a festival. The next weekend, we
had planned to see the doctor because Linda had felt a lump
she had never noticed before. They discovered that it was
cancer. Of course that was a devastating moment. You can be
a strong Christian with strong faith and know God can do
miracles and have a good repertoire of promises to glean

from, but when the doctor sits down in the chair across from you and looks you in the eye and says your wife has cancer, it still hits you real hard.

Human nature being what it is, we tend to project immediately into worst-case scenarios. I remember sitting there thinking, *Is this it? Is Linda going to live? How much cancer is there? Is it all through her body?*

It's hard now to remember a time when really I knew so little about cancer, which I think is true for a lot of people. You hear about cancer. I can remember seeing people in different places who were bald and pale and I would wonder if the cancer did that. I would hear about chemotherapy and didn't really know what it was or what radiation treatments were. They are words you hear and see reported on TV, and all of a sudden it's in your house.

Q: **How severe was the cancer?**

It had spread somewhat. We went down to the M.D. Anderson Research Hospital in Houston. Upon their testings and the biopsy they felt that a six-month course of chemotherapy and a mastectomy was the best treatment. During surgery they discovered the cancer was not contained. Which is why they did the chemotherapy.

Q: **So the surgery was your first big hurdle together?**

I knew it would be a devastating experience. Linda would have a large scar. No muscle. Not much tissue. It's pretty disfiguring. But I remember when the wrap came off the first time after about 10 days in the hospital and we both looked at the scar. I just told her, I said, "You bear on your body the marks of the Lord Jesus." Now, some might say, "That's really out of context." But our belief is that all the events of our lives, if we are in Christ, are either caused by or allowed by the Lord. And there is a purpose in all of it and there's a reason for all of it. And there is some identity at least in the sufferings of Christ when we go through the times of pain. My wife is such a wonderfully godly woman. We didn't understand it in the natural. But I was telling her there is a reason why you bear this scar, there's a reason why you're going through this. And Christ may not give the explanation in a sudden answer, but throughout the course of your life you will come to an understanding that this is how it translates into ministry, into compassion for others, into understanding in other people's lives who are enduring a similar trial.

Q: How did you deal with the chemotherapy that Linda still faced?

The doctors' announcement about the chemo was tough to accept at first. Chemo was a total unknown. Everything we had ever heard about it was disastrous. Sick all the time, sores in your mouth, lose your hair. It hits your body and organs pretty hard. So when the doctor said, "chemo," that was a two-by-four across the face. But you hit those moments of shock and then you kind of regroup and say, "OK, here's where we're headed now."

Linda basically would take a treatment for three days and then be off for three weeks. Chemotherapy is, in effect, killing all the cells in your body. In theory, at least, the good cells recreate themselves and the bad cells are killed off. Cancer that has spread can be anywhere in your body. So they hit your whole body with chemo to kill any undetected cancer.

Linda actually tolerated the chemo very well. The first couple of treatments she got kind of sick. I think it was a couple of weeks to the day after we started that she got up in the morning and she said, "Dallas, look." And there were clumps of hair lying on her pillow.

Q: How did she cope with that?

You know, the Lord gave these wonderful, little refreshing moments along the way. I remember when her hair started coming out, she just looked at me one morning and she said,

"They pulled Christ's beard out of His face. This doesn't hurt. It's just falling out. But they pulled His beard out."

Q: What would you say is the central lesson Linda's cancer has taken you both through?

We say casually that God is the most important Person in the world to us, or that we want to be like Jesus, but we don't really think those statements through too deeply sometimes. If we really want to please the Lord, there is a real clear-cut definition in Scripture of how that occurs. You've got to have faith, and faith by its very nature must be tested. Think of Job. Here's a righteous man, a man of whom God himself says, "Have you considered My servant, Job?" God never contests that Job is a righteous man. But Job has everything stripped from him — his possessions, his family and his reputation. He finally is afflicted physically and in pain. His friends and his wife show up and he gets the wonderful counsel, "Why don't you just curse God and die?" And in the midst of this overwhelming tragedy, it surely can't make any logical sense to him at all. But he says, "I know that my Redeemer lives and though He slay me I will trust Him." That's faith. That's the point God wants to get us to.

Q: Earlier you said you and Linda discovered "for the first time" in 1987 that she had cancer. That wasn't the end of it, was it?

No. In 1989 she discovered a very small lump on the other side. It was not a related cancer. It had contained cancerous cells. But because of her history the doctors said they needed to be very aggressive. She did not have to go through chemo that time, but she did endure another mastectomy.

Q: How did you deal with that, especially after having sought God to heal her from the first cancer?

I can remember praying sometimes and just thinking, *How many times do I pray the same prayer?* You almost get to a point where you don't want to pray because you feel phony about it. You've asked God the same thing over and over and it gets discouraging. You think you really can't make that much difference. And then something happens. You read something in His Word, or someone comes along and says, "Let me pray with you." There were times when Linda and I would sit down and, for whatever reason, God in His great mercy would allow us one of those breakthrough moments. And I can't explain that, but all of us have had those times. It's kind of like fishing. You go to your favorite hole one day and you load the boat up with fish. You go the next day and you can't get a bite. And sometimes in prayer it seems like you can't get a bite and then all of a sudden you go to the same place and you do it the same way and you load the boat up with God's goodness. Who can explain that?

Q: **So, if prayers seem to be answered one day and ignored the next, what do you do?**

Well, I can assure you prayers are never ignored. But how God responds to prayer is often beyond our understanding. I constantly tell people that God is up to things in our lives we know nothing about. Oswald Chambers says that sometimes it looks like God is missing the mark, but really we're too shortsighted to see where He's aiming. I just love that. It's so true. Sometimes in our valley and in our sorrow we believe if we just knew what God was doing that would settle it. I'm not sure that would make any difference. Faith is when you don't know. When it doesn't make sense. When you can't understand. But you trust in God.

Q: **What does faith mean to you?**

It's really a mystery. I think it's easier to tell you what faith is not. Some people have what I call a "hyper-faith persuasion." They don't process experiences like Linda's and mine very well. They tell you, "God just ought to heal that, and if He doesn't there's just something wrong with your faith." I believe some of these people are brothers and sisters in Christ, but they're misguided. If God says, "The thing I want out of you is your faith and the only way I'm going to get the faith I want is to test it," then to say, on the other hand, "Oh no, faith is a tool to get what you want," well that's totally opposed. No, God says, "Faith is to get what I want out of you whatever the cost."

Q: **When it comes to physical illness, there are some who say there should always be a healing at some point.**

Dedicated believers die of sickness. I lost one of my best friends to cancer. I lost my father two years ago to a long and difficult ordeal with cancer. As the old song says, "This world is not my home, I'm just passing through." We're not made for this world. This is a proving ground, a dress rehearsal. Where we're going will be perfect, but this idea that we're to live in perfection here is quite contrary to what Scripture teaches.

Is God a miracle-working God? Absolutely. Do we have the right to ask Him for a miracle? Absolutely. He says to come boldly, to run right into His presence and tell Him what we want and what we need and that He will pay attention to every word of it. But the Bible says, "Many are the afflictions of the righteous." That shoots the idea that if we're righteous we shouldn't have any problems. Jesus said, "In this world you will have tribulation." That's a done deal. Now, He does go on to say that He will deliver us out of them all. But we want to tack on one little extra word to that promise. We want Jesus to say, "I will deliver you out of them all … now." We think God needs to do what He needs to do the way we think He needs to do it. And then we think He needs to do it on our time schedule.

Q: **What did you and Linda discover as you continued to pray?**

When you graduate from a self-focused understanding of

prayer — "Oh, God, I need this" or "Heal me" or "Deliver me" — you discover, like Oswald Chambers said, that prayer isn't about getting things from God, though it does involve that. Rather, prayer is primarily about getting God himself. That is why we need to persist and continue to pray. It's not that God didn't hear us the first time. He knew what we were going to deal with before we ever prayed our first prayer. But as we continue to come into His presence, the most intimate dimension of our relationship occurs in prayer. When we're blessed and everything's fine, we can take it for granted and our prayer life can slide a little bit. But bring on adversity. Let the doctor sit down, look you in the eye and say, "Your wife's got cancer." The first place you find yourself is on your knees.

Q: Some people would wonder how you can trust God after all of this.

We trust Him more today than we did 15 years ago. You know, in the past, each time the doctor told us about Linda's cancer I would sit there in a clammy sweat, feeling a shock to my faith. But when the doctor gave us the news this last time, it was like, OK, God has been faithful and I understand now that these things happen for a reason. God is going to get us through it. God is going to be faithful. There is a dimension of faith now that I have that I didn't have even six months ago. I haven't arrived, and there's more to discover, but I'm moving on. I don't think we ever get to the point where we are no longer concerned about anything. But I don't sit around fretting over that worst-case scenario. In fact, Linda and I are in a whole new chapter of ministry. We minister together in all our concerts and in church services and we just released an album of hymns we did together called *Foundations*. She sings a solo on the album as well, and it's a real expression of everything we've gone through. We chose hymns that have supported us during some tough times over the past 15 years. God is so faithful.

— *Scott Harrup*

Asa Hutchinson
Drug Enforcement's top enforcer

Asa Hutchinson began serving as director of the U.S. Drug Enforcement Administration, the federal government's law-enforcement arm to battle illegal drugs, in August 2001. Hutchinson served as a lawyer in Arkansas for 21 years before being elected to the U.S. House of Representatives.

Q: **In what way is drug enforcement a good-versus-evil situation?**

When you look at the founding fathers or the preamble to the Constitution, one of the first principles of our government was to establish justice. It is essential for the goodness of America that we have law enforcement and we are a nation under the rule of law. That's what separates us from anarchy and really gives the framework for democracy to work and freedom to survive.

Q: **How has terrorism changed drug enforcement?**

It has given more responsibility to the DEA. Drugs are not just illegal and harmful; now we know they are a means to fund terrorism.

Q: What role do parents play in preventing drug abuse by children?

Parents are not just the first line of defense, but really the only defense. If parents don't exercise responsibility, we're just plugging holes. Drug use among teenagers is diminished when parents have meals with them once a day, spend time with them, talk to them and go to church with them on Sunday.

Q: What role do Christian rehabilitation programs such as Teen Challenge play in the anti-drug effort?

The treatment programs that involve the faith-based community are the ones with the most success, whether you're talking about alcohol addiction or methamphetamine addiction. It's difficult to overcome without some component of faith.

Q: Why is there an attraction to drugs such as Ecstasy?

The draw for those who traffic in it is the huge profit. You can make an Ecstasy pill for 25 cents and sell it on the street for $25. When it is targeted to young people, young people sometimes like to live on the margins and take risks. It creates enormous health consequences and it can be deadly.

Q: In some quarters there is a growing sentiment that certain drugs, especially marijuana, should be decriminalized. Why is that not a good idea?

Marijuana is a harmful substance. We underestimate the damage that can be done by marijuana. The level of THC, the addictive substance in marijuana, is much higher now than it was in the 1970s and therefore it's much more dangerous. I wish those who talk about legalizing marijuana could come with me to Judge [James] Doyle's courtroom outside Chicago [in Kane County]. He asked 15 heroin addicts how they started and they all said they started with marijuana.

Q: Does the amount of legal medication we take have anything to do with how we view illegal drugs?

There is a connection there. Prescription drugs are subject to being abused, but they serve a legitimate purpose and we want to make sure they are available for those who are suffering. But when teenagers see prescription drugs and then they see an Ecstasy pill, somehow they think it's not as harmful as a heroin dose. It's a real education challenge for us. The addict population is misusing painkillers, especially OxyContin. As an opiate substitute it's simply a new way to get the same drug.

Q: Is the term "drug war" a misnomer? Will we ever win such a battle?

To those in the law-enforcement trenches it's very dangerous and it's a war in many respects. But when you think of war, it has a beginning and an end. The fact is, there will always be illegal drugs from generation to generation. As long as there are depression, greed and teenagers, there will be a challenge.

Q: Is drug abuse only a teenage problem?

I have seen many people who are addicted still struggling in their 40s and 50s. Recently I saw an accountant who was going through a difficult time and all of a sudden he became addicted to drugs at 50. Although the greatest challenge is with young people, no one is age exempt.

Q: How can Christians pray about drug enforcement?

I would encourage people to pray for the truth. There are a lot of myths out there. Those with an agenda of legalization argue that there's no success, when in fact there is a lot of success. They argue that marijuana is harmless, when in fact there is much danger. They argue that there are no new ideas and there are. We want the truth to be out there.

Also, people can pray for the safety of the brave men and women in law enforcement who are risking their lives every day.

And also for the sacrifice of those engaged in treatment and have such incredible ministry with young people, helping them to make right decisions.

Q: Talk about your own Christian faith.

I'm grateful that my parents instilled in me an appreciation for church and having a relationship with God as I was growing up. It has made a tremendous impact on my life and the values I developed. A pastor in rural Arkansas invested a great deal of energy in young people, and through his ministry my faith grew and set me on a stronger path through life.

— *John W. Kennedy*

James M. Inhofe
Serving Christ in the Senate

James M. Inhofe, R-Okla., has been a United States senator since 1994. He previously served four terms in the U.S. House of Representatives, served in the U.S. Army and has been a businessman for more than 30 years.

Q: **Talk about your personal journey to faith in Jesus Christ.**

I accepted Christ on September 22, 1988, at 2:30 in the afternoon in the Members' Dining Room in the United States Capitol. I was 54 years old. I always thought I had been a follower of Jesus and had accepted Him, then suddenly realized that that hadn't happened. All the burdens of life were shifted, and I said, "God, it's Your problem now." It worked.

Q: How has your relationship with Christ affected your role in government?

The Scriptures I always use are Acts 9:15 and Acts 2:42. Acts 9:15 is Jesus' intention for Paul the apostle to take His name to the Jews, Gentiles and kings. I have gone through

Acts with a pencil and circled all the times Paul talks about Jesus' name. Acts 2:42 talks about the fellowship of believers. I belong to the Senate prayer breakfast, which meets on a weekly basis. We do four things together: We eat together, pray together, fellowship together, and talk about the precepts of Jesus together.

I'm heavily involved in helping the poor in Africa, and I make it a point to follow the political philosophy of Jesus. As a United States senator, doors are open to me. I am able to visit any "king." I've adopted 12 countries all the way from Benin, Cote d'Ivoire, Togo, and Gabon in West Africa as far east as Uganda, Rwanda and Burundi. I'm planning to meet with nine presidents in Abidjan, Cote d'Ivoire. My focus will be to meet in the spirit of Jesus. I have seen presidents of warring countries sit down in the spirit of Jesus and as a result two major wars have stopped. We've had national prayer breakfasts in countries like Rwanda and Burundi where the presidents, the members of Parliament, the Supreme Court justices, the top business people and the leaders of the Hutus and Tutsis — tribes that have been [fighting] for decades — all came together.

My faith allows me to put my job into perspective. I no longer worry. I trust God. As a senator for Oklahoma, I am very much concerned with my committee responsibilities and all the other issues in which my constituents are interested. But I no longer worry. I do it all in the spirit of Christ. It's tempting for senators to look in the mirror and think of themselves as being one of the most important 100 people in America; but in reality, we're just servants of the people. And I trust God with my legislative goals and the issues that are important to my constituents.

Q: Some people say that Christians shouldn't be involved in the political process.

Well, the other side has always been involved. That's the problem we've had. All the atheists were involved. All those who fought against prayer in public schools were involved. Then all of a sudden Christians got involved and everyone became hysterical. If the good people stay out of politics, what's going to happen to politics?

Q: What key issues should Christians be interested in?

The most current issue is what's happening in the Middle East. My Web site, inhofe.senate.gov, includes a speech I made on the Senate floor on December 4, 2001. It addresses from a biblical perspective seven reasons why Israel is entitled to its land. I don't believe there is a single issue we deal with in government that hasn't been dealt with in the Scriptures. So when you are talking about issues like abortion, you can go to the Scriptures. Homosexuality? Go to the Scriptures. The need for a strong defense? Go to the Scriptures. I discovered this when I was elected to the House before I was in the Senate. It occurred to me when I was first elected in 1986 that there are no new problems. Things are answered in the Scriptures. Believers who serve in Congress need to regularly meet and talk to each other about what Jesus would do. Bill Bright founded some groups that do just that. Every Wednesday morning when we have our Senate prayer breakfast, I give the Scripture lesson. I usually develop it around current issues.

Q: Have you seen a change since 9/11 in the way Washington operates?

Absolutely, but not so much in the attitudes of senators as in the electorate at home. September 11 was a wake-up call for the American people. I think there is a resurgence of patriotism. We've seen the attendance at some churches double. September 11 is going to mark the end of what I have called in my speeches the "age of perversion in America." I believe that age began when we kicked God out of our schools in 1963. David Barton is a great guy whose research I use. He helped me with a message that I've been giving for a long time on how the history of this country shows that we were, in fact, one nation under God. When a judge or a legislator was sworn into a public office in the colonial days, part of the oath of office was, in effect, "I have read the Holy Scriptures, both the Old Testament and the New Testament, and I will run my office accordingly." People argue over the issue of church and state. Back then it was John Witherspoon who trained 85 of our founding fathers. He was president of Princeton University and he was a believer. He said that if you want to have a good, moral country you must elect good, moral people into public office and their private lives have to back up their public reputation.

Q: Do you see hope for reversing the decay in the American family?

I think so. What kind of behavior do you expect in the family when a secular government is taking over the upbringing of our kids so that parents don't have to take responsibility? I think families are waking up to their need to take a much larger role, and I think it is going to go along with the resurgence of morality in America. I believe that this change we are experiencing is going to boost the family. I'm personally committed to those principles. Kay and I have been married for close to 43 years. We have four kids and 11 grandkids so we know something about family.

Q: How can Christians support fellow believers in government?

Each reader has two senators and one congressman. They have a responsibility to find out — and it's easy to do — who their federal representatives are and how they vote on the issues. A number of organizations rate members of Congress as to their record on family values, the sanctity of life, and other issues that believers prioritize.

When a member of Congress is someone you can believe in, let him or her know of your support. The most frustrating thing for someone like me is to go to a town hall meeting and be asked a question like, "Why don't you do something about the military?" That person didn't research my position and recognize that I'm helping to lead the fight for a stronger national defense. So the most rewarding thing is when someone stands up and says, "I know what your voting record is on these issues, and I appreciate your hard work."

On the other hand, if you have someone who is against those values you hold dear, you need to get involved with someone else and start supporting that person's campaign. People should support candidates who more closely represent their points of view. So believers must get involved. There is a strong moral base in America, but it needs to get behind members of Congress, or candidates, who share their values. Believers need to realize it is their moral responsibility to get involved.

— Ken Horn

Denise Jones
Girls of Grace

*Point of Grace was formed more than a decade ago by Shelley Breen, Terry Jones, Heather Payne and **Denise Jones** when they were just out of college. They have one platinum and five gold albums to their credit, 24 consecutive No. 1 singles, 14 Dove Awards and two Grammy nods. The group's eighth album,* Girls of Grace, *is more than just a collection of worship songs. It's a conference, a devotional book, a journal, and most importantly a movement that Point of Grace hopes will become a life-changing event for teenage girls. Denise Jones spoke about the group's dream of influencing the decisions of a new generation of women.*

Q: How was God working in Point of Grace when this new ministry got started?

Point of Grace has been together 12 years now, and at about our 10th anniversary we took some time off to be in our home churches and attend women's Bible studies. During that time, God began to place in each of our hearts very different things. I was in a Bible study called Intimate

Issues that dealt with the sexual aspects of marriage. God really began to speak to me about communicating with young girls about this issue because the world presents so many warped views of what sex is and what marriage is.

At the same time Terry was mentoring and discipling a group of eighth-grade girls from her church. It was very evident that someone needed to speak honestly to these girls. God was also working in the same way with Heather and Shelley.

One day a mom told Terry, "You all are finally old enough that I trust you to teach my daughter these sorts of things. Yet you're still young enough that my daughter thinks you're cool." That clicked. It all came together and someone came up with the name Girls of Grace. It seemed so fitting to go along with the outstretched arm of Point of Grace.

Q: **What were the first steps in the Girls of Grace ministry?**

When we started out as Point of Grace, God had already placed in our hearts the desire to minister to teenage girls. In 1992, we joined hands with Mercy Ministries of America, a ministry for teenagers and young girls between the ages of 13–28. It deals with all kinds of issues whether it is unwanted pregnancy, anorexia, bulimia, abuse, depression or you name it. We all four were raised in godly families and felt very blessed, and we realized that one wrong turn and we could have ended up where these girls are now.

Q: **What is the concept behind Girls of Grace?**

We've taken ideas from teen girl magazines and books and found that there are three things that they consistently talk about — boys, family and friendships. We've added another: your personal walk with Jesus Christ.

We've stuck to a lot of Scripture, and it's important to hear what God has to say about subjects like sex. We just try and give girls some real practical stuff. Heather talks about having personal time with God. Shelley talks about respecting parents and the importance of family and Terry talks about healthy friendships.

Q: What do you do at a Girls of Grace conference?

Concerts just don't give us enough time to talk about important things. So we offer a Friday night concert and an all-day Saturday event. On Friday, we do a lot of praise and worship. Nancy from Mercy Ministries of America speaks, and she just flat out presents the gospel. She speaks to girls like they are adults and she doesn't baby them. Our purpose for doing that on Friday night is that we want girls to know up front where their relationship stands with Jesus Christ. When we talk about sex and dating and God's plan for their lives the next day, if they don't understand in the first place that there is a God who cares for them at every place in their lives, how can they believe the other things we have to tell them?

Q: What was your main struggle as a teen when it came down to your relationship with Christ?

In junior high I was very focused on my relationship with Christ and with my friends, and I wanted to bring them to church or to the Lord. By the time I got to high school I was very distracted by my relationship with my boyfriend and I was very involved with basketball. When I failed, it did not occur to me that it was because I didn't hear God's voice. I was so engulfed in my own desires.

Q: What areas do you see teen girls really struggling with today?

They struggle with identity mostly. Who they are. Who they are trying to please. It can show up in the way that they handle an eating disorder, maintain relationships or go about their day-to-day lives. We're all distracted by these things. We're all trying to impress the people around us — our parents, friends, peers, and ourselves.

Modesty is another big issue. These girls are bombarded with the world telling them what to wear and how to look "right." We do this little fashion show part of the conference with some of the girls from the local host church who are all different sizes and builds. We reinforce the idea that God has made us all beautiful. You can still look cool but dress in a way that shows everything that you do and everything that is in your heart is for God.

We have some great footage for the conference from fellow artists Michael W. Smith and Toby Mac who say that the first thing they loved about their wives is that their wives loved Jesus. The musicians comment that when they are at concerts and see girls dressed in an inappropriate way, they just have to turn away. It reinforces the idea that if girls really want a godly guy, they need to focus on their relationship with God and make that relationship shine through into every aspect of their lives.

Q: **What is the main dating advice you try to pass to the girls you speak with?**

In my dating experience I've realized that the real issue is a girl's heart — what's motivating her. It's when they step across the cafeteria and sit with someone who always sits alone, and they do that because of the love that God has placed in their hearts. It's when they serve their brother and sister and in some way help them with a chore, and not so that their brother will do something for them. When they have a heart for God, that's when everything else will fall into place.

Q: **What kind of results are you seeing from your conferences?**

We have done four and we have been blown away at the responses. We had 9,000 girls at our first conference. We had 3,000 in Denver. It was sold out and we turned away more than 2,000. We had 4,500 in Grand Rapids and were also

turning people away. We don't even reach these numbers when we do a concert. It just goes to show how much this is needed. One of the comments that I continue to get over and over from girls is, "No one ever tried to talk to me about these topics before."

Q: How have you seen girls' lives change?

Girls have come together to form their own Girls of Grace study groups. They are walking through these issues and encouraging each other. There have also been decisions for Christ. We try to connect girls with the local host-church sponsors or youth leaders who can continue to minister and walk the walk with them.

Q: What is your definition of a girl of grace?

A girl of grace is someone who really knows how much Jesus loves her, with all her faults and all her good. And because of that love, it outpours into every aspect of her life.

Q: Do you have any final thoughts?

First Timothy 4:12 says, "Don't let anyone look down on you because you are young, but set an example for the believers in speech, in life, in love, in faith and in purity." That's what we feel called to instill in the lives of the teen girls we minister to.

— *Amber Weigand-Buckley*

Napoleon Kaufman
Gridiron faith

*A Spirit-filled believer, **Napoleon Kaufman,** formerly a running back with the Oakland Raiders, was one of the top rushers in the NFL. In 1997, he was ordained as a minister in the Church of God in Christ.*

Q: **How is your faith challenged by life in the NFL?**

My pastor often says that we're on the front line. On game days, I'm surrounded by thousands of people who call me names, curse at me, even spit at me. In the locker room, I have to deal with guys who live with non-Christian views and do sinful things.

But in the midst of the challenges, I've found that I'm able to draw strength from God. The more I'm around sin, the more I'm thankful for what God has done in my life. And I'm not the only one. If you look around the league, you'll see that people in football are getting saved. Guys are seeing Christ in those of us that live for Him.

Q: **You often speak to children and youth groups. What message do you give?**

Rather than try to preach sermons at these kids, I usually just give my testimony. I'm reminded of the apostle Paul as he stood before King Agrippa in the Book of Acts — he gave his testimony of how God had changed his life. King Agrippa was so touched he almost set Paul free.

So when I speak at schools I tell about what my life was like before I was saved, and what it's like now. I tell students that God can change their lives, that God is a habit-breaker and He sets free those who are in bondage.

Q: **In what ways do you try to convey a Christlike witness to your teammates, coaches and opponents?**

It's no secret to the other guys what I believe, and they respect that. When I first got saved, I think I was a little overzealous in my witnessing. A lot of guys out there talk about faith, but don't live it. So I try to live right before them. When the guys on my team are having problems or spiritual concerns, they know who to come to. How you walk sends a powerful message.

Q: **The past two seasons [1996, 1997], you've been among the league leaders in rushing. Did you ever envision having this kind of success in the NFL?**

In a way, I did. Excelling in the NFL is a goal that I set many years ago, and deep down inside I always believed I could. Before I got saved, it was hard when I didn't have good days. I would constantly beat myself up if it looked like I wasn't going to make my goals. But now that I'm working for the Lord, I know everything that happens to me is in accordance with the will of God. The steps of a righteous man are ordered by the Lord. And just knowing that has brought me peace. Now, even if I have a bad game I can still rejoice.

Q: What do you plan to do in your post-football years?

I've learned that it matters not what I want to do, but what God wants me to do. He'll put me where He wants to put me. I just want to see people's lives changed; I want to see people get saved. Whether I'm a pastor, an evangelist, or a deacon, I just want to see people come to a saving knowledge of Jesus Christ.

Q: What's your favorite Bible verse?

"I am crucified with Christ: nevertheless I live; yet not I, but Christ liveth in me: and the life which I now live in the flesh I live by the faith of the Son of God, who loved me, and gave himself for me" (Galatians 2:20, KJV).

In order to receive the fullness of God in our lives we must die in order that Christ might live through us. Oftentimes people believe in Christ, but refuse to die to themselves. Christ only shines His righteousness through you if you die to your flesh.

— *James Bilton*

Lillie Knauls
Single and satisfied

*Gospel singer **Lillie Knauls** has been a part of the Assemblies of God for more than 30 years. She has ministered in song at five General Councils and appeared at the Fellowship's 2000 Celebration in Indianapolis. Single and in her 60s, Lillie often speaks to groups about the "gift of singleness."*

Q: **Tell me about your religious background.**

My mom told me the first place I ever went in life was church. I was saved and baptized in the Holy Spirit at a very young age. I joined the Assemblies of God more than 30 years ago because it was so similar in doctrine to the church I grew up in. I am pleased that, under the leadership of Brother Thomas Trask, the Assemblies of God is redigging the wells of revival and rekindling the fires of early Pentecost.

Q: **When were you called to music ministry?**

In the 1960s I was working at the telephone company and

singing with a choir in the San Francisco Bay Area — the Edwin Hawkins Singers. We recorded an album that ended up No. 1 on the Billboard charts for many weeks — "Oh, Happy Day." Shortly after that God called me to full-time music ministry. I hung up on Ma Bell and have been traveling the world full-time for the past 24 years as a "musicianary." During my farewell luncheon at the telephone company God gave me Matthew 6:26 as a promise that He would take care of me, and He has done that.

Q: How do you maintain your personal relationship with God as you travel the world?

I spend time each day in prayer and continually meditate on His Word as I listen to teaching and praise tapes and ask the Holy Spirit to direct my steps. For He indeed has a plan for my life according to Jeremiah 29:11.

Q: Did you always feel God called you to be single?

No. I was engaged once, but began to feel the relationship was not God's will. I broke it off and started dating again. After a while, I asked God to please give me my husband if it was His will for me to be married. And if He wanted me to be single, I asked Him to give me the gift of singleness. As time went by, I felt it was God's plan for me to have a season of singleness. I have a very happy life.

Q: Is there anything you'd like to say to single believers?

One of the main challenges of living the single life was the difficulty of letting my life be a witness for God while coping with my human emotions such as loneliness, frustration and anxiety. However, this has been conquered. I am now single and satisfied. I challenge all singles to concentrate on the happiness available right where they are. Please do not put off being happy while waiting for that mate. Happiness is a gift from God himself to both singles and married. First

Corinthians 7:7 says that to some He gives the gift of being happily single and to others the gift of being married.

Q: **How can the church better minister to singles?**

By not letting them be an isolated group. Especially on holidays, singles should be included in family settings. I always have been.

— *Ashli O'Connell*

CeCe Winans Love
Of Gospel and Grammys

*Even as a child **CeCe Winans** was a natural on stage. She had the voice, the look and the presence that seemed to move and touch people. The only problem was that she was a less-than-willing participant. If she had had it her way she would have been back in the choir singing along with her friends far from the spotlight. But one Sunday morning, after being forced by her parents to perform, she realized she was not just singing a song, she was leading people into the presence of God. Suddenly, the girl with the amazing voice not only had dreams for her future, she had a calling.*

CeCe is the eighth of 10 children and was the firstborn girl. She grew up in Detroit, but now lives in Nashville with her husband, Alvin Love, and their two teenage children. CeCe spoke about her musical heritage, where it has led her and life lessons she has learned.

Q: **Your parents had seven boys and then you. Were you the princess of the family?**

I am sure if you asked my brothers they'd say, "Yes." But what can I say? I guess I was a pleasant surprise for my mom.

Q: **With nine siblings, did you ever feel as though you didn't get enough attention from your parents?**

During my childhood there was never a dull moment — or even a quiet one, for that matter. My parents did a great job of giving everyone attention. They didn't have any favorites and they laid down the law. What went for one went for the other. That made it pretty simple. All I can say is that God worked it out for them. With that many kids it had to be God.

Q: **Tell me about your parents.**

My father did a lot of everything. He was a barber by trade, but he worked in a factory as well. He also sold cars, was a minister and somehow found enough time to coach athletic teams in the community.

He was always very busy. My mom was a medical transcriptionist between cleaning, cooking and all the other stuff mothers do.

Q: **How did you become a believer?**

We were raised in church. My mom and dad were strong believers, always involved in church and they demanded that we were too. Going to church was not a choice for us; we had to go. But because of that we all fell in love with God.

I fell in love with the Lord when I was 12. That was when I started to make decisions that told others I stood for the Lord. I had accepted Him years earlier, but at 12 is when I decided to follow Him, stand up to others who criticized me for it and walk in the faith.

Q: **When did you know you had a talent for singing?**

Singing was something everybody did in our family. At church a lot of my friends sang, too, and I heard better voices all the time. I knew I could sing, but I never thought I was anything special. When I started doing solos at the age of 8 while in church I discovered I could sing. I didn't want to sing, but I was made to sing by my parents. When I was 14, I realized it was more than just a gift of singing, it was a God-given gift of ministry. As I sang a solo one Sunday I saw the reaction of the people and I realized there was something to this that was bigger than I was. It was a ministry.

Q: Did you battle stage fright?

Somewhat. I was always much more comfortable being in the background. I have a family where half of us love being out front and half of us hate it. I am one who would have been happy to be in the choir or singing in the studio where no one could see me. But God had other plans.

Q: What was your professional debut?

My first recording session was with Andrae Crouch. My family had met him and we went to Los Angeles to record some songs with him. I made a little money, so I guess I became a professional then. But I really became a professional when my brother BeBe and I began performing on the *Praise the Lord* television program.

Q: Did the reception and ensuing success of your first album catch you off guard?

I was very surprised. When you go into the studio to do something you love to do and you're a young kid, you're not really expecting much. We were just excited about giving listeners the message of Jesus Christ through our songs. And we were just happy we were getting a chance to do it. But when people began opening their hearts and listening to what we were saying through our music, it really hit us.

Q: When you started becoming famous and making money did it have an adverse effect on you?

No. God has always blessed me by surrounding me with great people and by letting me be a part of a wonderful church. Those two elements have kept me on track. My family has, too. We're each other's greatest fans, but we'll let you know in a minute if your head has gotten too big.

Q: What obstacles have accompanied your success?

Some people say I've sold out because I've had mainstream success. Other people have said things about me because of the money I've made. There will always be critics, but being misunderstood is the worst thing because I can't explain everything to everyone. I just have to trust that God is going to take care of me.

Q: Let's talk about your mainstream success — have you ever regretted not concentrating all your efforts that way?

I don't regret it at all. First of all I wasn't called to do that. But God has proven that He can take whatever He wants and allow it to cross barriers and spill over into the mainstream even when I don't plan it. The success BeBe and I have had in the mainstream has been exciting because we have had a chance to share the good news with a lot of people who need it. My calling is to bring light to a dark world, not add more darkness.

Q: In 1995 you and BeBe decided to pursue solo careers. Why?

It was the best move for both of us because it was God's will. That's the only way I can describe it because I hated the idea of performing by myself. But again, God had another place for me. He wanted to teach me more about himself. I know now that BeBe and I have both grown separately in different ways. But I really do long for the day when we can get back together.

Q: How many children do you have?

Only two. I come from a family with 10 children so I feel like I cheated. But we had a boy and a girl and it was like, "Hey, we're done."

Q: **What's a lesson you learned from your parents that you hope to pass on to your children?**

By far it is to live the Christian life at all times. My mom and dad did not just teach us about the Lord, they lived a holy life in front of us. That is the biggest and best example I've ever had.

Now I strive to do that daily with my children. I try to teach them God's way and stress the importance of having God first in their lives because that is guaranteed success. No matter where you are or what you do, if you love the Lord then you're successful.

Q: **What have your kids taught you about faith and parenting?**

To stay on my knees. Don't get me wrong, we have two great kids. But my main prayer for them has always been that they would both love the Lord. And they do.

Q: **What have you and your husband discovered to be the key to a strong marriage?**

Alvin and I know what it takes to make a marriage work and to live a fulfilled life: Jesus. We know we're going to have rough times, but Jesus is always ready to help fix things as long as we keep Him at the center of our marriage.

We've been married for 19 years. We've had a few rough times, but when you both love the Lord you consult Him on what you're going through. And when you listen to the Lord you stay together. People try to make it difficult, but it's not. Flesh has to die. We have to take up our cross.

Alvin and I haven't had a lot of rough times because we really enjoy each other's company. We believe in spending time together and we love going to church and having God at the center of our marriage. But when problems do arise we handle them the way the Word tells us to.

Q: **Dispel a couple myths about the "glamorous" life you live.**

As far as everything being picture-perfect, it isn't. Look at my album covers. I've heard people say, "You look so cute," and I just laugh. I look good on those things because they have worked on my makeup and hair all day.

Q: **So what is reality for you?**

My life is not perfect. Not at all. But God is always perfect. He is my Source and my Life. Without Him I would be crazy. If He told me to stop singing tomorrow, I know I would be OK because I have Him in my heart.

Q: **How do you keep your relationship with the Lord fresh and new?**

I spend time with Him. For me it's not an option. I have to put Him first. It's so important to be rooted in His presence by studying His Word and praying without ceasing and fasting. You have to do everything He tells you to do because that's the only way to become a strong disciple.

Doing so helps me stay focused on who I really am and on what my purpose is. Without Him I am nothing. Without Him I will die. He is my Source, my Life, my Joy and my Peace.

Q: **When you get to the end of your life, what do you hope people remember the most about you?**

I hope they say, "She was just like Jesus." That's what I strive for. But I don't strive to be like that for people — I strive to be like that for Him.

— *Kirk Noonan*

Josh McDowell
Is the Bible true?

*Since 1964, **Josh McDowell** has been a traveling representative for Campus Crusade for Christ. He heads the Josh McDowell Ministry international organization located in Richardson, Texas. He has spoken to more than 7 million young people in 84 countries, including visits to 700 university and college campuses. McDowell is the author or co-author of more than 75 books. Among his most popular books are several offering clear defenses for the Christian faith:* New Evidence That Demands a Verdict, More Than a Carpenter, *and* Right From Wrong: What You Need To Know To Help Youth Make Right Choices.

Q: How has Christ changed your life?

After I set out to refute Christianity intellectually and couldn't, I came to the conclusion the Bible was true and Jesus Christ was God's Son. On December 19, 1959, at 8:30 at night I placed my trust in Christ as Savior and Lord and asked Him to come into my life and forgive me.

Over time things began to change. Where I once constantly lost my temper, I found myself arriving at a crisis and experiencing peace. Where I once believed people were there to be used, I started thinking of other people first. I once had a lot of hatred, mainly toward my father, an alcoholic. I despised him. After I came to Christ, I could look my father in the eyes and say, "I love you." That shook him up after some of the things I had done. As a result, it brought him to Christ also.

Q: **Some might say that your testimony is just subjective experience. What makes a Christian's claims more valid than those of a Buddhist or atheist, for example?**

I always ask people, "What is the objective basis for the subjective experience?" I am not a Christian because God changed my life; I am a Christian because of my convictions about who Jesus Christ is. He is the Son of God. He died on a cross for my sin, was buried, was literally raised from the dead on the third day.

Q: **What distinguishes the Bible from other religious works?**

It is a book that is based in history with historical evidence and data. In Luke 3, for example, there are eight or nine historical references in the first verse. The Bible is not just a theological dissertation; it's a theological dissertation set within history that can be checked out.

I once thought all I had to do was refute Christ's philosophy and my case was won. But I came front to front with history — with a Person named Jesus Christ, with a book called the Bible that was based within history.

Another difference is in the message of the Bible — that man is sinful, man has fallen and there is nothing man can do to get out of it without God taking the initiative to reach him. That message separates the Bible from so much other religious literature.

Finally, the Bible presents God becoming Man. Its whole message is revolutionary.

I wrote a book, *Jesus: A Biblical Defense of His Deity,* because the deity of Christ is found from Genesis to Revelation. Several passages in the Gospels are some of the strongest. For example, in Mark 2:5, Jesus said to a paralytic, "Son, your sins are forgiven" (NASB). Now, whenever you read any historical document, you always read it in light of the historical context. When you consider the audience He spoke to and the meaning in that context, it was a bold statement.

We're commanded to forgive others who wrong us, but Jesus took a person who had sinned against God the Father and said, "I forgive you." Immediately the Jews said, "Why does this man speak that way? He is blaspheming. Who can forgive sins but God alone?" And Jesus said, "That's right. I forgive you." That's one of the boldest claims to deity.

John 10:29,30 talks about Jesus' sheep. Jesus says, "My Father, who has given them to me, is greater than all; no one is able to snatch them out of my Father's hand. I and the Father are one." You might say, "I and the Father are one" in spirit. But that's not what Jesus said in the context of His audience. He said, "I and the Father are one" in essence and meaning. Look how the Jews, Jesus' audience, responded. They picked up stones to stone Him. And Jesus answered: "I have shown you many great miracles from the Father. For which of these do you stone me?" (v. 32). And the Jews answered Him, "We are not stoning you for any of these … but for blasphemy, because you, a mere man, claim to be God" (v. 33). To the audience He was addressing, Jesus made a direct claim to deity.

Those are two of about 40 related passages.

Q: **Why are Christ's claims valid?**

My presupposition is that Jesus' claims are valid because He is God in human flesh. But Jesus said, "If you do not believe me for my words only, at least believe me for the sake of the miracles that I have done." He said, "The blind see, the lame walk, the sick are healed." Christ confirmed His message, as did the disciples, through miracles and healing.

Christ also fulfilled prophecy, substantiating His claims. I have a whole section in my books on 333 messianic prophecies in the Old Testament all fulfilled in one Person, Jesus Christ.

Another point would be how Jesus appealed to the Father and gave credit to the Father and stated He was God in human flesh. The Resurrection was probably the biggest proof. I recently did an interview for an Easter special on CBS on the Resurrection. I went over and over how the Resurrection confirms that Jesus Christ is the Son of God. And here is what is unique and even makes the Bible different from other books: Other people claim to have been raised from the dead, but their power is always from someone else. Jesus claimed He had the power to raise himself from the dead and His followers would be raised from the dead. That's a unique claim in the literature of religion.

Q: **Some say Christ's disciples made up the story of His resurrection. Is there evidence of the Resurrection?**

Here's the simplest answer: Within weeks, the disciples proclaimed the resurrection of Jesus Christ, that He had been bodily raised from the dead and appeared to them. Where did they do that? Jerusalem. Where did the Resurrection allegedly take place? Jerusalem. If they had connived a scheme, and Christ had not been raised from the dead, where would have been the hardest place on the face of the earth to convince anyone? In Jerusalem. A 15-minute walk would have exposed the body in the tomb. They preached it in the hardest place in the world to convince anyone that Christ had been raised from the dead if it was a fraud.

Q: **How can one Person's death 2,000 years ago change someone's life in the 21st century?**

If Jesus was not who He claimed to be — the Messiah, the Son of God, the Redeemer — then it couldn't. He might be a model for you, a motivation. If you study the life of Abraham Lincoln, you might live for others and take bold stands. But Jesus claimed to be God. He claimed that unless we are personally related to Him we are still in our sins and we are not saved.

If Jesus Christ was who He claimed to be, and He did die on a cross at a point of time in history, then, for all history past and all history future it is relevant because that is the very focal point for forgiveness and redemption. So, a Person who died on a cross for the sins of humanity has an impact on a person's life today in forgiveness.

Second, Jesus not only died on the cross for sins, but also was buried and raised from the dead, ascended to heaven and sent the Holy Spirit. Because Christ lives, 2,000 years later He has that capacity to enter a man's or a woman's life and to change that life from the inside out. Jesus is relevant in forgiveness and through indwelling power.

Q: **In your travels what continuing evidence do you see of Christ's influence on the world?**

One of the biggest is the impact through His followers in compassion for the hurting — like the Convoy of Hope. I wish every denomination had a ministry like that. Convoy of Hope, Operation Carelift, Samaritan's Purse, World Vision — everywhere I go there are demonstrations.

And there's the power of forgiveness that I see in so many believers in some of the most heart-wrenching situations.

Then there is the growth of the Church. In some of the most difficult parts of the world people are responding to Christ in spite of the circumstances, showing the power of God at work today.

— Scott Harrup

Matt McPherson
Doing business by the Golden Rule

Matt McPherson is founder and CEO of Mathews Inc. and McPherson Guitars. Mathews has become a premier producer of compound bows and is internationally recognized in the archery world. McPherson Guitars creates high-end acoustic instruments praised by a growing number of professional musicians. But for McPherson, no professional accomplishment can overshadow the priority of his relationship with Jesus Christ; no corporate title can compare with simply being called "Dad."

Q: **You have stated that your faith is the foundation for everything you have accomplished. When did you give your heart to the Lord?**

I was introduced to Christ at a very early age. My father was an Assemblies of God minister. As far back as I can remember my mom prayed the prayer of salvation with us. I was around 4 when I accepted Christ as my Savior.

Q: **The success of Mathews Inc., your parent company, has been phenomenal. How did you become involved in creating bows?**

My father became an archer shortly after my parents were married because my mom wasn't comfortable with guns. Dad introduced my brother, Randy, and me to bow hunting. Money was tight and if you wanted something badly enough you made it. So I cut down small saplings on my parents' property and started building bows very young. Dad ended up buying Randy and me 20-pound yellow fiberglass Ben Pearson bows. Those were our first serious bows. We got more involved in archery as we got into junior high and high school. Randy and I talked to the shop teacher and asked if we could manufacture bows. So we started making bows at that time.

Q: **What about McPherson Guitars?**

I started playing acoustic guitar probably around 1975. Dad and Randy were guitar players as well. Dad would buy a guitar and handcraft some changes on it and listen to it. Around 1980 he came up with a design that had three sound holes and he was pretty pleased with that. He contacted me and said he felt this was a guitar that needed to be produced. I had always wanted to build guitars. So I got some books on how to build guitars and used the new direction that Dad wanted to take and melded the old technology with the new.

Q: **With two corporations and numerous other projects, how do you manage to keep business, family and faith in balance?**

It's not easy, especially at first when you are starting something out and there is a tremendous amount of effort to actually get the momentum that you need to make a company successful. But it's like eating ice cream. I like ice cream; but if all I eat is ice cream, I'm going to get sick. It's the same thing with the business world. If all I do is business, I'm going to end up having a marriage that is not successful. My life doesn't revolve around my business. It revolves around, first of all, my personal relationship with God, and second of all, my wife and my family. There were definitely a lot of hours to put in the first years of the company, but there was always a way to set aside time for my family. Now, God has blessed and I'm able to spend a lot more time with my wife and three sons.

Q: What fathering principles can you share with other businessmen?

It is very important to a man that he provides for his family. But my advice is, if you want to keep that in balance with relating to your family, listen to your wife. Sherry would periodically call and say, "Honey, I need you home." And I would say, "I've got to get this thing done." And she would say, "Honey, I need you home. You haven't spent enough time with the kids and I need you home." And I realized she was serious. I would put everything down and go home. Husbands can get too focused. Wives look at the whole picture.

Q: What are some principles that serve as a foundation for how you do business?

"Do unto others as you would have them do unto you" is by far the simplest and most practical form of doing business that I can possibly imagine. When I do business in a way that I would like to have somebody do business with me, it is always a winner. When I'm going to market a product, I look at it from the points of view of the retailers who sell it and the consumers who buy it. If you give product value to everybody involved in the process, including your company, it is always successful. I've never seen it not successful. My goal is to see everyone along the line get treated fairly.

Q: **What would you say to a person who claims that you can't get ahead in business if you limit yourself to biblical principles?**

I'd say, first of all, if the industry you are in can only succeed by being untruthful, you have to get a new career. I refuse to lie. I remember a long time ago we had a problem with shipping our product. I told our people to always be straight up with our customers. If they called, we needed to admit we messed up on this. We thought we could get it out but we weren't able to on time. I have found that when you are honest it may take longer sometimes, but when you are done you don't have a house that is built upon sand. You have a house that is built upon a rock.

I once had someone tell me that a little dishonesty never hurt anybody and that I would never get ahead unless I was willing to compromise. I told that person, "If it is the last thing I do, I hope to prove that wrong." As far as I know, that person is still eking out a living while God has wonderfully blessed our people. There are a lot of people in the industry who know that if I tell them something it doesn't have to be on paper. And that's worth something in the business world.

Q: **Have there ever been times where you faced crises and you had to rely entirely on God?**

Many times, but here's just one example. There was a new model bow I had built one year. Throughout all the cycle testing that I did, it held up and everything looked fine. But there was an issue that came up in the actual production of this bow that was a serious problem if I couldn't fix it. "God," I prayed, "this could really hurt us if I can't figure out how to bring this to market. I can't ship these bows until I work this out, and we've got orders for them." God helped me find the solution the same day. It was amazing. I was able to design the part that I needed and have it manufactured. We proved that it worked and we were up and running within a week.

Q: Is there anything else you want to add?

If your heart truly is to serve God and you are doing things with integrity, then God will bless. I believe you will be able to reach more people for Christ than you ever dreamed possible.

— Hal Donaldson

Terry Meeuwsen
Putting family first

Since 1993, **Terry Meeuwsen** *has served as Pat Robertson's cohost of* The 700 Club *on the Christian Broadcasting Network (CBN). A former Miss America, Meeuwsen has had successful careers as a broadcaster, author and recording artist. At home she is Mom to Drew, Tory, J.P. and Tyler. She spoke about her most treasured responsibilities: wife and mother.*

Q: **What have been the most challenging roles of your life?**

I don't even have to think about that: wife and mother. These roles touch everything that you do. Biblically, after my relationship with the Lord, those are my next priorities. The secret to both is to have a servant's attitude. That's true with everything we do, but it's harder to maintain that under your own roof than it is with the world. I know that a dad has a huge responsibility in leading the family, but the mom really sets the tone. If I am out of sorts, it's really like that saying, "If Momma ain't happy, ain't nobody happy." It affects my whole household. God has given both that responsibility and that privilege to me as a woman.

Q: How do you balance your public ministry with your responsibilities as wife and mother?

One of the blessings for me is that CBN is very committed to family. When they asked me to come here eight years ago, I questioned the Lord. I loved being an at-home mom, and I had no desire to go back to work full time. I said, "Lord, why would You ask me to do this when my children are still young?" And I felt like the Lord told me that my children were part of the reason I was going.

But I still had a lot of anxiety. Pat Robertson had never had a cohost who was a mother. And it's different when you have someone who is a mom. Nothing goes the way it is supposed to. Life is just one spontaneous moment after another. But from the very beginning CBN has been incredibly positive toward my family needs.

Q: And you're a homeschooling mom?

Yes, I am homeschooling one of my sons. Often while I do the program, he's doing his homework in my office. And then we're able to have lunch together and then I take him home. So I have an unusual scenario here that would not necessarily be available to me in another workplace.

Q: Tell me about your longtime dream to adopt a Korean child and how that dream was finally realized.

I would like to explain clearly why I had that desire, but I'm not really sure myself. It was something that was in me for many years. When I met my husband, Andy, and we knew we were going to be married, he adopted my dream as his own. The process took several years, and J.P. came to our home after the birth of our first two children. He was such a gift. All of our children have been incredible gifts — just to be able to have children is an incredible blessing. God blessed us so abundantly. We were off the charts with gratitude.

Q: **Your fourth child is also adopted. How did that come about?**

The desire of our hearts was to have four children. I am the oldest of four; Andy is the oldest of four. We had discussed how great it would be to adopt again. And we had even thought we'd like to adopt a black or biracial child, but we never asked God for a fourth child because we felt that He had already so abundantly blessed us.

A friend of ours met a 20-year-old woman who had recently become pregnant. This girl was frantic over her circumstances. She had been told her child would never be accepted because he was neither black nor white. Our friend told her about J.P. and how he had been so wanted and so loved and accepted. And she said if she could find a family like ours, she would place her child for adoption.

So we're eating dinner one night and our friend calls. Not knowing about our desire, she asked if we would consider adopting a biracial baby. Well, we almost swallowed our forks. We were just ecstatic. We were there when Tyler was born. It was just a great, great blessing and a gift from the Lord. He really completed our family.

Q: **What would you say to couples who desire to adopt a child but are discouraged by the process?**

First, pray and ask God to lead you. He knows the desires of your heart and heaven knows there are many children in need of families. God will make a way where there seems to be no way. Begin the process and see how God opens the doors. It's a great adventure to walk with the Lord through these places when we can't see the end. Those are the times when we get into the flow of the Holy Spirit and embark on a God adventure.

And there are wonderful opportunities to adopt special-needs kids. Not just kids who have profound mental and physical disabilities, but also kids who might need cleft palate surgery or maybe a heart surgery or who might have a hand that's missing a finger or two. In their cultures, these children would have no chance for a normal life, but in America they would have incredible opportunity. You don't have to be a person of great means to do this. You just have to be a person who is willing to embark on an adventure and who has a lot of capacity for love. God can make the impossible possible.

Q: **Having a career in the public eye, you're well aware of how image-conscious our society can be. How can we raise our children to find their self-worth in Christ?**

Welcome to every Christian parent's greatest challenge — I really think that's the hardest thing to do with your kids because everything in our society and our culture is working against you.

Having two adopted children I especially want my kids to find their identity in Christ and know who they are in Him before they know any other aspect of who they are.

Parents can help children do this by walking through the Scriptures with them, helping them discover God's purposes for them. And pray. Pray more than you talk. Pray for your children. Pray with your children. When I put my kids to bed at night, I physically lay my hands on them and pray.

Children need to know that in the everydayness of life and growing up Mom and Dad are thinking of them and praying for them. They just need to know that they are covered.

Q: **You have the opportunity to talk to so many fascinating people. What's the best advice you've received about raising a godly family?**

Pat Robertson has given me a lot of godly advice in numerous ways. Just working with him and hearing how he raised his kids has impacted my family. I've listened to his kids say the thing they most remember is getting up in the morning to find him reading the Word every day. I once asked his son, Gordon, "What is the most memorable thing that your dad ever taught you growing up?" And he said it was to stay "blessable." God wants to bless you. If we're not in a position where God is able to bless us, it's by our own choosing. I have really stressed that with my kids.

Q: **You bring your viewers a message of hope and inspiration daily. Where do you turn to be inspired and encouraged?**

I go to the Lord. My favorite time of the day is after everyone is asleep and I can brew a cup of tea and just sit down with the Lord, maybe read the Scriptures, maybe read a book that God is using to speak to me, maybe listen to some praise and worship music, maybe write in my journal.

And I have good Christian friends. I think this is so important. God uses us to support each other and refresh each other and keep each other accountable. Some people find that in their church or in a cell group or in a Mom's-in-Touch group. It doesn't matter where. What matters is that you're plugged in somewhere.

Q: **Anything else?**

We live in very challenging times. We have to be vigilant about our commitment and our walk with the Lord. We have to be vigilant about our marriages and our parenting. We live in a dying world, and we've got the answer. We're the torchbearers. We need to share that light with gusto, understanding that the opportunity is a privilege.

— *Ashli O'Connell*

Dr. Bernard Nathanson
A former abortionist speaks out

Bernard Nathanson, M.D., once headed the Western world's largest abortion clinic. In the mid-'80s, as a proclaimed atheist, he became pro-life and produced and narrated The Silent Scream, *showing abortion from the victim's vantage point. Dr. Nathanson is now a devoted follower of Jesus Christ.*

Q: **When you presided over some 60,000 abortions, what kind of mental struggle was going on — having been trained in the Jewish religion?**

There was no mental struggle. I was doing exactly what I thought was right at the time. I was not a practicing Jew. I was Jewish, of course, but not practicing religion.

I was convinced in the face of the scientific evidence and the social sciences that we were doing the correct thing — we were helping women, we were saving women's lives from illegal abortionists. And that conviction stayed with me until such time as we began to understand a good deal more about the human fetus and particularly after we had a window into the womb with ultrasound and all the rest.

Only at that time — this was after I had left the clinic — did I begin to have some doubts about what we had been doing and then gradually stopped doing abortions in my own private practice. But during my tenure in the clinic, I had no mental struggles or any kind of ambiguity about it.

Q: How has this country fallen to where it is now — both morally and ethically?

I'm a bioethicist, as well as a physician. I just finished a graduate degree in bioethics at Vanderbilt University. Why do we sanction abortion and active killing at the end of life or physician-assisted suicide or cloning or genetic manipulation or all these technologies which basically distort the image of man — the image of how God made us and what we should be?

The answer is that, I suppose for the last 50 years or so, there has been an increasing emphasis on what is called autonomy ... that we are in charge of our own bodies and our own minds. Now that concept is fine in theory, and it certainly is important. But it has been elevated to the level of a deity. It has been deified to the extent that it is now bereft, sliced away from all other considerations such as community ties, family ties, church ties, national ties, anything.

Children indoctrinated with this idea of autonomy — "You can do your own thing," or however you want to phrase it — are not told that there must be certain restraints on that autonomy and those restraints are those communitarian ties I spoke of. What's gone wrong with this country now, morally and ethically, is that autonomy has run rampant. It has become perverted and it has become enshrined. So everybody does what he or she wants.

That goes from one end of life to the other — abortion and the use of fetal tissue to treat adult disease and for fetal experimentation, all the way over to active killing and physician-assisted suicide. The courts have allowed autonomy and self-governance to run riot, unrestrained. Until that is repaired —

until that concept has been wiped away and a more reasonable and more ethical and more moral concept of autonomy is developed — we are going to be wallowing in these problems.

Q: So what hope do you see in all this?

Interestingly, there are spots on the horizon that are very encouraging. For example, Dr. Willard Gaylin, a psychiatrist — who used to be president of the very liberal Hastings Center, which is probably the most prestigious bioethical institute in this country — wrote a book called *The Perversion of Autonomy* in which he expressed these very thoughts.

Various little pockets of resistance are beginning to spring up to this idea of unrestrained autonomy. And I think that in the end we will come to a sober realization that autonomy — this unrestrained, do-your-own-thing quasi-philosophy — is destructive, evil, and must be stopped.

Q: What would be the most effective use of a Christian's time in these battles — say the abortion issue?

Of course, prayer. The most vital thing we can do is pray.

The second thing is to teach our children, our young people, that they have stronger allegiances than the allegiance to self. They have allegiances to God and to their families and to their teachers and to their country and to everything that is outside of their own scope.

If we indoctrinate them with this idea, we are going to get people who believe in the importance of community and God and life. We are not going to get kids running rampant who victimize people and hold them up for drugs and all the rest of it.

Q: You found Jesus Christ as your Savior several years ago and you were baptized in water. Who is Jesus to you?

Oh ... such a question. Jesus encompasses everything that is good and right and merciful and forgiving and beautiful and loving. If you are living a life that is not centered around Jesus, your life is not worth anything.

I must tell you this: For many years I thought I could control my life, as most of us do. When I looked back some years ago, all I saw in my wake were broken lives and wasted opportunities and material acquisitions that were rusting and nothing of value. Nothing of value. I suddenly realized my life had spun out of control and I just simply could not, I was not wise enough, to control it. No one is.

The only Person whom you can turn your life over to with firm, beautiful confidence that it will be a good decent life is Jesus. That's all. Nobody else.

— Ann Floyd

Janette Oke
Writing for the Lord

*Author **Janette Oke's** first book, a prairie love story called* Love Comes Softly, *was published in 1979 by Bethany House Publishers. Since then she has written more than 75 others with sales now topping some 20 million copies. She lives in Calgary, Alberta, Canada.*

Q: When did you first know you had a talent for writing?

Even as a very small child — before I could actually put the words down — I would make up stories verbally. I always enjoyed writing assignments in school and promised myself that someday I would try it.

I had wanted to have some training because I feel that, as a Christian, I should do everything to the best of my ability. But that didn't happen.

The years were ticking by. My four children were in their teens when I decided that, if I was ever going to do it, I was going to have to dive in. With a great deal of prayer I did. *Love Comes Softly* was the result. The only writing I did before *Love Comes Softly* was just a few magazine articles.

Q: **The time period you write about is pre-Janette Oke. Where do you get your information?**

My favorite period has always been the time of the frontier pioneers. So I read everything Western I could find as a teenager.

I was born and raised in Alberta, so the area I lived in still had some of the original settlers living there. And my parents came to the provinces as children, so I heard a lot of stories of what it was like in those days. By the time I was ready to write, I had a good background, both through hearing personal accounts and through reading.

One thing that impressed me about the pioneers was that so many of them came West with a very personal faith. And the church in the community usually reflected the nationality of the immigrants. So we found that our small towns are almost identified by the oldest church as far as who the settlers were. Yet, this is seldom addressed in cowboy stories.

Settling of the Canadian West happened in a little different way from settling of the U.S., but there's quite a bit of carryover as well.

Q: **The secular media says we have to show and tell everything in its rawest form, because that's life. But you're able, with sensitivity, to develop characters who experience real life. Is there a formula or philosophy you apply to handle this kind of tension?**

I make no apologies whatever for not including what the secular world may say is absolutely necessary. As a Christian community, we have every right to provide alternative reading. Writing is just another extension, another expression of my life. I wouldn't be involved in any of that, so why should I be writing any of that?

Q: **Talk about your personal relationship with Jesus.**

I don't know how anyone gets along in life without a close relationship with the Lord. I accepted Him as my Savior when I was 10. I had been brought up in a home with a Christian mom and had gone to church and Sunday School and vacation Bible school prior to that. But it wasn't until I was 10 that I discovered that I had to make the choice to ask for forgiveness for my own sins.

My writing has helped me to grow considerably in my faith. I know that I have to depend on help from God for every book I write. Writing has been a wonderful way for me to sort through my faith. As my characters go through struggles and try to solidify and share their faith, I have to do that along with them.

I have had readers challenge me — readers whose faith is a bit different from mine. Then I go back to the Scriptures and ask, "OK, why do I believe this?" I have had some wonderful search-throughs.

Q: **What would you like to say to today's woman about her children, her home, her husband?**

There is no higher calling than being a wife and mother. We see so much tearing apart of the home today. This is one of Satan's biggest attacks. Hopefully, we see a little swinging back the other way.

I was listening to a program about young women and the very horrid crimes they are now committing. They are getting into things that were normally known to be the man's world — stabbings, victimizing, etc. And these psychologists from the secular world commented that this is a backlash because these young women did not receive adequate support in their homes when they were young.

The secular world is realizing that something has gone awry. We in the Christian community need to be very conscious of this in raising our children. We can be the salvation of the nation in the future. This is within our capability. We can't legislate change of heart. We can't legislate morality. It has to come from training.

And we as wives and mothers — particularly as mothers — this is our responsibility. It's a big job, but it's a very rewarding one. If we see the future wrapped up in each one of these little ones, we see what a wonderful privilege and responsibility we've been given.

Remember that marriage is a partnership. My husband is academic dean at a Bible college and my primary concern is to support him in his ministry.

Q: Anything else?

Whatever you have, whatever you are, give it all to God. He can do the most exciting things with your life — far beyond what you would ever dream — if it's completely given to Him.

— Ann Floyd

John Olerud
Hope when your health fails

John Olerud is an all-star first baseman for the Seattle Mariners, earning two Gold Glove Awards. He's played in three World Series, two with Toronto and one with the New York Mets. Olerud nearly died from a brain aneurysm while in college, and his 2-year-old daughter was born with a birth defect that has prevented her from walking. He talked about the hardships Christians can face.

Q: **You were holding your daughter while nurses worked on her in the hospital. Talk about how that reminded you of a Christian's relationship with God.**

I think the thing that jumped out to me is sometimes we have questions about why we're going through things. We ask, "Why are we suffering and why are things going like this?" My daughter was getting poked. Here she was in what she'd thought were safe hands. And I'm letting them poke her. I think a lot of times as Christians we think, *God, what is going on? If You're there, why are You letting me get poked?* For me, I was looking down at my daughter, saying, "You need to get these antibodies and you need to get all these fluids in you." That's what was best for her. I knew there was no reason to explain because she wasn't going to understand anyway. That hit home. During our sufferings, our trials, we're praying the same way: "Lord, I don't understand what's going on. Do something about this." And I'm sure He's up there saying, "Love to explain it to you, but you wouldn't understand. This is just something you have to do. Trust Me."

Q: So, being a Christian doesn't mean saying goodbye to problems?

Absolutely not. That's how we're made mature and complete. The Book of James has been a big help for me. God uses trials to make us more mature and complete. That's part of our growing. Ultimately, there is going to be prosperity when we get to heaven. It's going to be unbelievable. But in this life, if you're thinking you're going to get everything you want in life you're going to sour on Christianity because there are going to be trials. If you think it's nothing but good times and blessings, you're going to come up saying, "This Christianity thing isn't true because I'm getting hammered here."

Q: Did your aneurysm change your perspective on life?

Definitely. I realized I'm not in control of things as much as I thought I was.

Q: Do you think your recovery from your aneurysm was miraculous?

I think the whole thing was miraculous. It was miraculous that the aneurysm leaked just enough where I had a grand mal seizure that sent me to the hospital. They searched for a problem, couldn't find it and sent me back to school. Just before I got back to exercising and running, my dad (who is a doctor) called me back to the University of Washington for more study. They found the aneurysm; they did the surgery. It was a lower-risk surgery because I had a month to heal (from the aneurysm) and get stronger. Everything went smoothly. I was back playing baseball in a couple of weeks. I didn't have to go through rehab, learning to walk and talk like so many other people do. I think it's definitely a miracle.

Q: How's your Christian walk?

It's an ongoing process. Christ is going to be working on me. He's the One who is going to do the perfecting. Not me. That's a good thing.

— *Gail Wood*

Stormie Omartian
Recovering from abuse

Stormie Omartian is a popular speaker, musician and author of numerous Christian best sellers. She and her husband, Michael, have enjoyed a longstanding ministry as Christian artists, producing records, videos, books and other resources. Stormie spoke about the challenges of relating to an abusive mother and her discovery that God can bring healing in the most trying circumstances.

Q: **Your childhood was difficult. Could you talk about some of the pain you faced?**

I was raised on an isolated ranch in Wyoming in a home without running water or central heat. My mother was mentally ill and my dad was gone a lot. Even when he was home, Dad was so tired that he barely seemed to be there. Mom was always talking to the voices in her head and she would put me in the closet to punish me, although I never was sure why I was being punished. If I protested in any way, however, I'd really get punished. Often, she forgot I was in the closet. Our house was old, so there were mice and spiders and once there was a snake. The dirty laundry was kept in that closet, so I spent the hours sitting on the laundry basket pulling my feet up so nothing would crawl over them. I was very afraid and I believed that life was hopeless and futile.

We moved when I was older. Mom no longer locked me in the closet, but she continued to be abusive and referred to me in the most obscene manner. When I went to school and was able to visit friends' houses, I realized for the first time just how abnormal my home life was. Mom was so unpredictable; she could become violent at any time. So I never brought friends to my house. This only intensified my feelings of isolation and lack of love.

As an outgrowth of those experiences I tried to kill myself when I was 14. As I grew older, I relied heavily on alcohol and drugs and I became involved in unhealthy relationships. I delved into Eastern religions and the occult. I was trying to find some way to dull my pain. Whatever I tried would seem to work temporarily, but ended up sending me into deeper pain. There was always a backlash.

Q: How did you come to Christ?

At 28, I was at the end of my rope. I'd tried everything there was to try to beat my pain. I felt I couldn't live any longer. I planned my suicide more carefully this time, hoping it would look like an accident. A friend I was doing a recording session with noticed my depression and insisted that I meet with her pastor, Jack Hayford of Church on the Way in Van Nuys, Calif. The three of us met at a restaurant. He talked with me a long time about Jesus Christ, and he made the gospel come alive for me for the first time in my life. He gave me three books to read: the Gospel of John, C.S. Lewis's *The Screwtape Letters* and a book on the working of the Holy Spirit. I went home and read them. My eyes were opened. I know people must have been praying for me because the words just seemed to leap off the page. We met Pastor Jack the following week in his office. I accepted Christ as my Savior that day in October of 1970. It's been nearly 32 wonderful years.

Q: **Several of your books focus on the power of prayer. How has prayer transformed your relationship with the Lord and with loved ones?**

Prayer has saved my life. My husband, Michael, and I were married in 1973. Between my salvation experience and finding a marriage partner, my life had turned around. I believed that all of my problems would be solved. But I still struggled with long-term bouts of depression. Going to church regularly and studying the Bible were helping, but I had not yet identified my depression as something that needed to go. Several pastors' wives were really gifted in helping people who were depressed. I began to attend counseling sessions at my church and it was eye-opening to discover that I did not have to live with those feelings.

My counselor fasted and prayed with me and helped me see that God had a different plan for my life. A big part of my recovery was confessing my unforgiveness of my mother and asking God to set me free to forgive her. As I prayed, I felt my depression lift from me. It was like someone removed a crushing load from my shoulders. I had discovered the power of prayer. I began to wonder what else God could do in response to prayer. I discovered that God wants us to pray and to partner with Him to see His divine plans enacted. When we realize how prayer can affect our marriages and our children and our work and our relationships, we can begin to bring God into those situations in a deeper way. There are so many things we just don't think to pray about, and God waits for our prayers to act in our behalf in those areas.

Q: **What advice do you have for mothers?**

A mother has tremendous power and authority in prayer over her children. I would tell any mother to always remember she has that authority and power and that God is on her side. What she nails down in prayer will be set by the power of God. When she prays against the enemy and says, "You are not getting my child; I claim this child for the kingdom of God," and then prays over every stage of that child's life, it is amazing what happens. I know a lot of parents get intimidated with their children, especially if a child becomes rebellious. And a rebellious spirit is intimidating. But parents need to recognize that that rebellion is not of God and that they do not have to stand for it. In prayer they need to go to battle for their children.

As wives, women also need to hold up their husbands in prayer. They need to take authority over the enemy's attacks on their partner and break down spiritual strongholds that might endanger their marriage.

Q: Having come through a difficult relationship with your mother, how have you seen God at work in your own years of parenting?

My children are grown. Christopher, 25, is a musician and record producer. John David, 22, married recently. He and his wife, Rebekah, bought a home near us and we're so excited about that. We adopted John David when he lost his parents. His mom was my best friend in high school. Amanda is 21 and in college. I prayed over them all even before they were born. I was a prayer partner with John David's mom when she was expecting him. And I prayed over them every day they were growing up. Prayer preempted a lot of issues we might have faced otherwise. There were some battles. My children, coming up in a family of musicians, would not always discern the kind of music they should listen to. We'd have to take some CDs away on occasion and pull down a few posters of music groups. But God preserved them from so many things. And to this day, I still pray for my children that no one will ever influence them away from the Lord.

— *Scott Harrup*

Barry Palser
Columbine's eternal impact

Barry Palser, associate pastor of Resurrection Fellowship in Loveland, Colo., spoke about the spiritual impact of the 1999 school shootings in Littleton. Palser was one of three pastors who officiated at Rachel Scott's funeral, broadcast worldwide by CNN and the Fox network.

Q: **Tell us about the youth group in your church — the one Rachel Scott was part of.**

Our youth group is passionate — the kids are really into evangelism and discipleship. We go after unsaved kids; and when they're saved, we get them into discipleship groups. One of our youth pastors, Lori Johnson, is a graduate of Columbine High School.

Now the kids who were lukewarm in their spiritual experience are saying, "You know what? I'm making my mind up right now I'm going to live for Christ. I'll die for Christ."

They are the heroes in all that is happening — these young people and their youth pastors.

Q: **So, you're seeing people commit or recommit their lives to Christ.**

Clement Park has become a memorial. There are cards, signs and flowers — thousands of them. We send our kids there every day to witness and win people for Jesus Christ. Their feeling is that if Rachel would give her life and shed her blood for Jesus Christ, who cares what others may say.

The presence and anointing of God were at Rachel's funeral. Now we're hearing reports of people around the country whose eyes were glued to the television, weeping openly. A church in Delaware called and said that night they had a memorial service for our children. Their church of 750 was packed; 150 people came forward to receive Christ.

Q: **You've been on the scene from the beginning. Put these events in some broader perspective.**

History shows that when Christians give their lives for Jesus, there is a harvest of souls because it shakes the Christians out of their lukewarmness. When you're serious with God, sacrifice is not an issue.

We see these deaths as martyrdom. Eyewitnesses said Rachel received four gunshot wounds. Before the fatal shot, the gunman asked if she believed in God. Rachel answered yes and the gunman said, "Then go be with Him."

We believe we have a window of opportunity and we should do anything we can to build up the body of Christ. We have sown seeds of godlessness in our children and in our nation; now we are reaping it. Pastor Bruce Porter said government took prayer out of school, but the kids put it back in school on Tuesday, April 20.

A news reporter interviewed a student who said, "When the bullets started flying, I hit the floor and started praying and speaking in tongues."

Another student said the gunmen asked her if she believed in God and she said, "Yes, I do. That's what my parents taught me" — she was quoted in the Rocky Mountain News — and they shot her six times but she lived. These kids are so bold for Christ.

Q: Is this a wake-up call for Christians?

I think it certainly is. If a tragedy of this magnitude cannot awaken us, we must be in bad shape. I have read secular articles that have said that our nation could very well experience a spiritual awakening. If media outside the church are saying this, then how much more should Christians proclaim it. It is time for churches and congregations to focus on the harvest. Now people are even more open to receive the gospel. They are confused, scared and looking for answers. The church of Jesus Christ has the answer.

— Kirk Noonan

Chonda Pierce
A time to laugh

*Christian comedienne, author and recording artist **Chonda Pierce** has endured more than her share of pain and loss but has found healing through laughter. Often compared to the queen of clean comedy, Minnie Pearl, Chonda appears regularly on the Grand Old Opry Stage in Nashville, Tenn., and tours frequently throughout the United States.*

Q: How did your experiences growing up as a preacher's kid contribute to what you do today?

They contribute greatly. For one thing, a lot of those fun stories from church end up being great material. Preachers' kids learn to sing in the choir, teach Sunday School and clean the bathrooms before we're 4 years old. So being in front of people all my life was a great blessing.

Q: You've had your share of heartache, including your parents' divorce and the deaths of your two sisters. Did you use humor as a coping mechanism?

I can't say that after the deaths of my sisters I just snapped and decided to cover everything up with humor. My father went through bouts of depression my whole life, even before my sisters passed away, so I had already known how to cover up difficulty. When my sisters died and my parents divorced, that hurt. So then I learned to cover up pain. And it made the recovery process even more difficult.

Ecclesiastes says there is a time to laugh and a time to cry. We have to learn when the right time is. When you don't know when the right time is, you laugh inappropriately. No one can laugh all the time.

Q: How did you get your start in comedy?

A theme park called Opryland USA was in Nashville for years and years and was one of the best places for a teenager in Nashville to get a good job — a clean place to work, reasonable hours, good pay. I tried out for one of the shows. The first year I didn't make it. I found out later it was because I was too skinny — oh, how I'd love to have those years back.

So I auditioned again the next year, and I got hired. The only way I could keep my job was to impersonate Minnie Pearl, because it was the one job in the show that would excuse me from the big dance number, which I was terrible at. And so in God's providence I got a part in a show where five times a day, seven days a week, I had to make people laugh. It was at a time when I didn't feel like life was very funny.

Q: So this job began a healing process for you?

You know how you just float along in a fog or a haze just trying to get through the days? That's what grief does. It just hangs like a cloud for a while. And in that cloud of grief, in order to make a living and to pay my college tuition, I got a job making people laugh. I got to experience firsthand what it means in Proverbs that laughter doeth good like medicine. It was medicine for me first. It changed everything — from not only a healing process that began but also an eye-opener to performing. I found that I loved hearing people laugh much more than the applause after I sang. I fell in love with comedy.

Q: **Tell me about your relationship with Minnie Pearl.**

Miss Minnie was a fan of the young people at Opryland. She would encourage them in their performance interests. One day my boss said to me, "Sarah Cannon would like to meet you after the show. She thinks you did a good job." At the time I didn't even know that Sarah Cannon was Minnie Pearl.

She thought I did a pretty good likeness of impersonating her and had a good sense of timing, so I started getting a little extra work impersonating her on the side. Down through the years, I would do events with her, and we had a little routine going.

The Holy Spirit really used her to speak to me. One night backstage she asked me if I liked this kind of thing, and I said, "Yes, ma'am, I do. I really like this."

And she said, "Well, honey, you'll never really know what laughter is until you make peace with God and know Him first." I'm certain that as a godly woman she could sense the anger and the bitterness and that cutting edge that sometimes you get when you're unhappy.

Q: **What is life like in the Pierce home?**

My son is a big cutup and seems to know no strangers. My daughter is more serious. She takes after her father. I grew up in a Nazarene church, and my husband grew up Southern Baptist. Now we go to a Pentecostal church. We have a diverse life. I'm real excited that, because the Holy Spirit is such a part of our lives, our home doesn't have a whole lot of sarcasm in it. That's a sweet, sweet reprieve. I remember how lonely it can feel when you're using laughter in an unhealthy way.

Q: **To what do you attribute the rise of comedy as a ministry venue?**

The term Christian comedienne raises eyebrows for people

who need to give Christianity a new look and another chance. For those of us who need a new way to evangelize, comedy is appealing. It's appealing even nationwide. Just like the rise of sitcoms on TV.

That is the nationwide appeal to humor. I'm really grateful and excited that the church embraces this idea as well because who should be happier in the world than we are? We know how the story ends; we're heading home. Now it doesn't mean we don't have problems and we don't grieve or have struggles, but in our spirits we're free.

Q: Anything else?

My pastor and my mother have been two of the most incredible people at teaching me to be salt and light in a dark world. As a comedienne and a Christian entertainer, I get more work in the corporate world and on national TV because the world is generally pretty sick of the vulgar stuff. My pastor has been good to help me accept the role that God has given me to be salt and light in an odd way. It's a precious gift that I don't take for granted.

— Ashli O'Connell

Steve Pike
A candid discussion about Mormonism

The Church of Jesus Christ of Latter-day Saints, known commonly as the Mormon Church, is often acknowledged for its successful missionary program. Mormon men, at the age of 19, are expected to spend two years serving their church. Many Mormon women also serve at the age of 21 for 18 months. The church claims to have more than 60,000 missionaries serving in at least 162 countries.

Steve Pike, director of church planting and development for the Rocky Mountain District of the Assemblies of God, offered insights on dealing with Mormon missionaries. Pike served for 10 years as a church planter and pastor in Utah, where he cofounded Project Exodus, a ministry aimed at freeing victims of false-faith groups in America.

Q: Why do you believe Mormonism is so appealing to people today?

Over the past 15 years or so, the LDS church has successfully transitioned itself from being viewed as a fringe cult group to being accepted by many Christian groups as a legitimate denomination under the broad umbrella of Christianity. As a result, many Christians now view the LDS church as a "sister" organization with only minor doctrinal differences from Bible-based Christian groups.

The average person who encounters Mormon missionaries or members no longer views them as a group to be avoided, but rather a legitimate religious group to be considered. And, the fact is, when theological concerns are removed, the LDS church is very attractive.

Among other benefits, joining the LDS church provides a person with a strong social support network that isn't always found in Bible-based Christian churches. The LDS church also has enjoyed amazing success at developing lay leadership throughout its organizational structure. Its short-term missions program is unparalleled by any traditional Christian group. And the LDS church has excelled at humanitarian efforts over the world. All these assets and more make the LDS church very attractive to the people of this generation who tend to be less concerned whether a religion is true and more concerned with whether it is good.

Q: What do Christians need to know about LDS missionaries?

Most LDS missionaries are very young and relatively inexperienced. As such, they are generally kind young people who are giving up what many consider to be the prime of their lives in service to their church. They are primarily interested in conducting "discussions" with interested seekers, rather than engaging in debate with seasoned saints.

They are usually a long way from home and serve with someone they have known for a relatively short period of time. They are involved in constant activity six days a week. They have limited contact with their families. With all this in mind, we should remember to treat them with "gentleness and respect" (1 Peter 3:15) and understand that the best thing we can do for them is to help them see Jesus in us.

Q: **What mistakes do Christians make when confronted by LDS missionaries?**

The two most common mistakes are rebuke and debate. "Rebuke" has to do with the idea that if we tell them they are wrong using strong statements from Scripture that the missionaries will "wake up," realize the error of their ways and turn away from their deception.

"Debate" is based on the idea that a logical presentation of scriptural facts will demolish their belief system and lead them to salvation. Both these approaches are usually unproductive in leading an LDS person to faith in Christ.

Since LDS people are taught that Bible-based Christians have some of the truth but not all of it, it is easy to see why rebuke and/or debate responses just don't work very well. Witnessing to an LDS person is usually much more of a process than an event.

We need to pray that the Holy Spirit will use us over time to help them begin to see through the veil of deception (2 Corinthians 4:4) and discover that salvation comes by grace through faith, not by works, so that no one can boast (Ephesians 2:8,9). This process simply takes prayer, time, anointed communication and authentic relationship.

Q: **Some Christians invite Mormon missionaries to their homes hoping to turn the tables and witness to the missionaries. Do you advise this?**

Yes and no. No, if you simply want to argue with them, embarrass them or prove them wrong. Yes, if you want to enter into a process of redemptive relationship that will help the LDS missionaries discover God's grace demonstrated in the person of Jesus.

Many people choose not to invite LDS people into their homes because of the admonition of the apostle John in 2 John 1:10: "If anyone comes to you and does not bring this teaching, do not take him into your house or welcome him."

It does sound like he is saying that we should not even let a person like a Mormon into our house.

However, it is important to remember that there were no "Holiday Inns" in those days.

I believe that John was admonishing believers to avoid providing a place to stay for those who taught false doctrine. I don't believe John was forbidding inviting them into your home to share the love of Christ. However, it is generally a good idea to have other believers with you when you invite LDS folks in. If you are alone when they come for the first time, invite them to come back. Prepare for their visit with prayer and by inviting other believers to be a part of your meeting with them. And plan on a "redemptive relationship," not just a one-time encounter.

The first stage is building a relationship. Relationship will be followed by thoughtful discussion. Eventually, when an appropriate level of trust and understanding is achieved, it may be appropriate to challenge their doctrinal assumptions in a manner that is more confrontational. I have found that LDS people are willing to listen to me, even when I say things that are hard for them to hear, if they know that I truly care about them.

Q: **What advice would you give to someone who is considering joining the Mormon Church?**

I would invite them to look before they leap. They should carefully study the Gospels and Paul's writings in the New Testament and see how these Scriptures compare to the teachings of the LDS church. They should recognize that although the LDS church has invested great effort in presenting themselves as another Christian denomination, the core LDS beliefs create a huge gap between the LDS church and Bible-based Christian groups.

They must also realize that LDS members are expected to proclaim without apology that the human organization headquartered in Salt Lake City, Utah, is the "One True

Church authorized by God." They will be expected to agree that Christ's church ceased to exist from around A.D. 100 until 1830 when God restored His church through a young man named Joseph Smith. They must realize that many of the core LDS teachings are not shared with members until after they have been baptized and participate in sacred rites in the LDS Temple.

Many resources regarding Mormonism are available from Gospel Publishing House or from local Christian bookstores to help seekers make a fully informed decision about the LDS church.

— Ashli O'Connell

Jay Sekulow
Religious liberty and justice for all

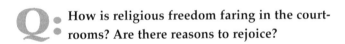

Jay Sekulow *is chief counsel for the American Center for Law and Justice in Virginia Beach, Va. The ACLJ engages in litigation, provides legal services, renders advice and counsels clients, and supports attorneys who are involved in defending the religious and civil liberties of Americans. It is a nonprofit organization that does not charge for its legal services.*

Q: **How is religious freedom faring in the courtrooms? Are there reasons to rejoice?**

There certainly are. God has been extremely gracious to us and others engaged in the struggle for religious liberty. During this decade we have argued and won several major cases before the U.S. Supreme Court dealing with public distribution of religious literature, Bible clubs in public schools, the right to conduct peaceful pro-life demonstrations, and free-speech issues. Regarding Bible clubs, we have gone from less than 500 clubs in the U.S. in 1990 to now more than 15,000. In cases such as these the American Civil Liberties Union and People for the American Way have had to agree with our arguments, albeit reluctantly.

169

Q: **What trends in American law give you hope?**

Increasingly, the Supreme Court and the lower courts understand that in this country Christians have the right to speak out on public issues. For example, it is becoming more acceptable for students who want to offer a public prayer or religious speech at a graduation ceremony to do so as a constitutional right. I am very optimistic on that front.

Q: **How do you respond to people who disdain the legal system as cumbersome and ineffective and say, "Why bother; nothing will change"?**

I point them to the Old Testament example of Nehemiah. He served in the king's court and knew how to utilize the secular institutions to accomplish God's purposes for His people. Our job is to utilize those same institutions to obtain justice for God's people today.

Q: **How should Christians concerned about law and justice pray and act?**

Caseloads have reached an all-time high. Although we are seeing great victories in the courtrooms, the struggle for religious liberty continues. Recently a student from Ohio called me about a Fellowship of Christian Athletes group on his public school campus. The group was told to remove the word "Christian" from their club name. So the battles are raging full force. We need wisdom. We need more people to be watchful in their communities and stand up for religious freedom, particularly in the public school.

Q: **What steps should individual Christians or churches take when their civil or religious liberties are attacked?**

First, don't be afraid to stand up and demand your rights as a citizen of the United States. Remember, Paul demanded his rights as a citizen of Rome. Also, do not be intimidated by those who oppose the Christian worldview. Understand that their anger is not directed at the messenger but at the gospel. Our job is to faithfully proclaim it.

For those who personally come under attack, the ACLJ is here to help. The ACLJ is a not-for-profit, public-interest law firm. Our services are free to people who contact us. Last year alone we received 102,000 requests for help or information.

When someone calls whose rights have been violated, we go to work for them in the courtrooms or city councils or wherever the venue is to protect their rights. Someone must answer groups like the ACLU. That is what God has called us to do. Presently, the ACLJ has full-time regional offices in six states. We have lawyers in every state — more than 500 attorneys affiliated with the ACLJ. We have also expanded internationally with offices in Russia, England and France.

— John Maempa

Michael W. Smith
Called to worship

*During the Assemblies of God's 50th General Council —
held in Washington, D.C., in 2003 — **Michael W. Smith** led
worship during the Turn America Sunday special gathering
on the Mall on August 3. Smith has been at the forefront of
contemporary Christian music for more than two decades
and has promoted worship concerts across America in recent
years.*

Q: **Tell us about your spiritual walk and what's
been happening in your life.**

I'm learning new stuff every day. It was really a new thing for
me to actually to do a worship record on a CD. I've been doing
worship for years. But I've never really done a whole worship
record on CD. We did that first worship album in Lakeland, Fla.,
and it took on a life of its own. It was one of the most extraordinary things I've ever been a part of. I think there is just something that, even if you listen to it today, it's power-punched.
God showed up big time and people had an encounter with
God and you get to experience it when you hear the CD.

Q: In light of the theme, Turn America Sunday, how do you think America needs to be turned?

I came back from a festival last night up in New Hampshire put on by Dan Russell. He has such a passion to get people out of our subculture a little bit and to challenge the church to be what the church is really supposed to be. I think we kind of get caught up in our little country club a little bit and so many of us don't even know who our neighbors are. What about the orphans and what about the widows? What about the people that are incarcerated? We don't seem to have time for those kinds of things. I feel like I'm supposed to be a part of not only challenging myself but challenging the church to wake up. We have got to get proactive and start living the life. It really is time for a spiritual revolution among the church.

Q: How do you hope to affect people with your music?

I have a heart to lead people into a real intimate encounter with God and I think it can happen through worship. Worship is more than just what happens on Sunday mornings. Worship is 24/7. It's a lifestyle. At the same time, I really have a heart for the lost and I think I still have some sort of platform to be able to reach out to a mainstream audience and hopefully to share the gospel with them.

Q: In your travels, do you see any encouraging signs of spiritual revival in today's culture?

I just got back from Europe. I spent three weeks there and it's just refreshing that there are people who really have a heart for God. There's this whole passion thing that's happening. That's what I'm encouraged about — seeing people getting their passion. It's contagious, an intense seeking after God. I didn't see that 10 years ago. I'm seeing it now. You look out and see an 8-year-old kid, hands raised in the air, weeping and crying and it's not just emotionalism. That's a refreshing thing to see.

— *Ken Horn*

Wayne Stayskal
On the drawing board

*Nationally syndicated editorial cartoonist **Wayne
Stayskal** is known for his unique cartooning style and ability
to drive home his point on some of the nation's most hotly
contested topics with his disarming humor. Stayskal, who
attends Victory Church (Assemblies of God) in Lakeland, Fla.
(Wayne Blackburn, pastor), spoke about life as an editorial
cartoonist.*

Q: How did your upbringing influence your decision to accept Christ as your Savior?

My parents were Christians and made sure I went to
church. I had a good foundation to build on and some good
Sunday School teachers, too. When I was 8 years old I was
baptized. Looking back now, I think I got baptized because
my older cousin was getting baptized and I wanted to do
what he did even though I had not yet accepted Christ as my
Savior. After that, whenever a pastor would give a call for
salvation, I would feel a tugging in my spirit to go forward,
but then I would think to myself, *I don't need to go forward; I've*

been baptized. While in the Air Force I met a Christian lieutenant who was training navigators for the Korean War. He held Bible studies and I attended them. One night during the study, it dawned on me that I was not saved. In my bunk that night, I asked the Lord to come into my heart. What a feeling that was; it was great. There was no mistake about it.

Q: Has cartooning been a pursuit of yours your entire life?

As a child I couldn't get by without a pencil in my hand all the time. Every Sunday I copied the comics from the newspaper — those cartoons were my inspiration. I tried to do my own cartoons, but I did better copying them at the time.

My folks caught on to my interest in art and sent me to a neighbor who taught oil painting. In high school, I took all of the art classes I could. After serving in the Air Force I went to the Chicago Academy of Fine Art. After I graduated, I was leaning toward cartooning, yet my cartooning career did not pan out as I had planned. For a year I worked in commercial art studios. After that I took a job at the *Chicago American* newspaper, where I did layouts for their Sunday magazine along with some cartoon illustrations.

Q: How long until you started doing cartoons full time?

It all started about two years later. I was now the art director for the Sunday magazine. I heard about a big publishing company looking for an art director for their encyclopedia's yearbook. Down deep I just knew that job was mine, but when I applied I was turned down. I couldn't find out why I did not get it. God seemed to remind me that I never talked to Him about it. So I started talking to God about my career, and I told Him that I wouldn't try to control it anymore — I would just follow wherever He would lead me.

Soon after that, Vaughn Shoemaker, an editorial cartoonist and a two-time Pulitzer Prize winner, started working at our paper. He was also a Christian. He wanted an assistant and I got that job. I did it along with my art director duties. I also started a small editorial cartoon three times a week for the bottom of the editorial page. Vaughn gave me many good pointers along the way. When he retired 10 years later, I took his position as chief cartoonist. When the paper ceased publishing, I took a job at the *Chicago Tribune*.

Q: Your career and notoriety were starting to soar at the *Chicago Tribune*. Why did you leave?

I left there in 1984 when newspapers across the nation, including the *Tribune,* were having financial problems. We had three editorial cartoonists; the other two were Pulitzer Prize winners, so I had to go. They gave me a year to find another job. Just when I needed it, God worked it out so I could come to the *Tampa Tribune*.

Q: What are the main ingredients of a cogent editorial cartoon?

For me, number one is humor. It's the old "a spoonful of sugar makes the medicine go down" theory. Number two is to decide on the right thing to say. Three is to get my idea across as simply as possible.

Q: How do you keep from coming across as angry or spiteful in your cartoons?

I try to avoid it, but sometimes it's in me and comes out. I admit I got a bit heavy-handed during the Clinton years. All cartoonists get too close to the issue at times.

Q: Do people ever get angry with you for the cartoons you do?

People have protested against me in front of our offices. Some write letters or call. Sometimes when people call they yell, but after they stop yelling we talk and it generally ends up being quite friendly.

Q: Have you ever been threatened with the loss of your job over a cartoon?

No, but they have not used a cartoon from time to time. My boss always explains the reasons why he would rather not use it. When this happens, I just do another one. Fortunately, this doesn't happen often.

Q: Do you have a sense that you are defending something?

No, I wouldn't use the word *defending*. I think it is more pointing out what is right in a world full of so much wrong. The bottom line is, I'm just like everybody else voicing his or her opinions. Although I may seem to yell a little louder because I have the privilege of being amplified through syndication and Web sites.

— Kirk Noonan

Rebecca St. James
A family ministry

*In 2002, **Rebecca St. James** was named Best Female Artist by the readers of* CCM *and* Campus Life *magazines and by the listeners of K-Love and Air1 radio networks, and she released her fastest-selling album to date,* Worship God. *2003 brought the release of* Wait for Me: The Best from Rebecca St. James, *featuring 16 handpicked fan-favorite hits. St. James has traveled throughout the U.S., Australia, New Zealand and Canada and received numerous Dove Award nominations.*

Q: **Looking back to your fourth album, *Pray*, what song on that album moves you the most?**

I'm passionate about the title track especially when I sing it live. It came out of some humbling, breaking trials that I've been through recently where I felt God teaching me to trust Him. Through those experiences, God helped to break me. The song talks about humbling ourselves before God and praying. It's based on 2 Chronicles 7:14.

Q: **How has your career changed your relationship with God since your first release came out when you were 16?**

It's helped me mature earlier than I would have. Before I started singing, I was homeschooled. I cleaned houses and baby-sat every week. It was a different life but still more normal than most. My life now is very, very different. I'm away from home most of the time. I sing in front of people most nights, do interviews and write songs and books. I'm very grateful to be doing what I'm doing because I'm fulfilled and at peace. I was at peace cleaning houses when God called me to do that, and I'm very content doing this.

Q: **What have you learned from Q&A times with your concert audiences?**

I've been challenged with the idea of selfishness. What a big problem selfishness is with us as humans. I've seen where my generation is finally realizing that if you live for yourself, it's a dead-end street. God's way of giving our lives away is life.

Q: **You're privileged to work with your family. Introduce your six siblings and share how they minister with you on tour.**

My brother Daniel serves as our lighting director and occasional background vocalist. Ben helps with lighting. Joe helps with staging and background vocals. Luke runs a spotlight. Josh runs the other spotlight. Libby has sung with me on *Pray*.

Q: **What are some things that you've learned about family from your family?**

The importance of honesty. We have a family policy of no secrets. Mom and Dad really challenge us that we've got to be honest and open. So many young people have bought into the idea that parents don't understand — they're outdated.

We need to pursue relationship with parents and say, "Mom and Dad, we need to talk. I really need your input in my life."

Q: **How challenging is it to build relationships outside your family?**

Very challenging, because I'm so rarely home. I have some wonderful friends in Nashville who understand my life. Also, I'm privileged to have a friend on the road who helps keep me accountable.

Q: **What has God been laying on your heart recently?**

All of us at some time struggle with questions like, "Why is this happening?" Life can be hard. Just because we're Christians doesn't mean we're exempt from troubles. The fact that we are able to know the Creator of the world — it's such a joy and awesome privilege. There is hope, and that's Jesus. I want to share that with everyone who will listen.

— Matt Wilkie

Lee Strobel
The case for Christ

Lee Strobel received a bachelor of journalism degree from the University of Missouri-Columbia and a master of studies in law degree from Yale Law School before a 14-year newspaper career that included a stint as legal affairs editor of the Chicago Tribune. *After nearly two years of studying the life of Christ, Strobel became a Christian in 1981. His book* The Case for Christ: A Journalist's Personal Investigation of the Evidence for Jesus (Zondervan, 1998) *became a best seller. Now an author and evangelist, Strobel also has been a teaching pastor at two of the nation's largest churches, Willow Creek Community Church in South Barrington, Ill., and Saddleback Valley Community Church in Lake Forest, Calif.*

Q: Why did you write *The Case for Christ?*

I wanted to help seekers and other people who were far from God to understand the historical basis for Christianity. Having been an atheist myself and having suffered the consequences of living the atheistic lifestyle, I have a lot of empathy for people who are outside the family of God and are skeptical about the claims of Jesus. The book also is designed to help Christians solidify what they believe and dialogue with nonbelieving friends.

Q: **How did your background in investigative journalism and law help you in writing this book?**

It helped me formulate questions to consider what constitutes reliable and persuasive evidence and to compile the case for Christ in a cumulative way that demonstrates the overall arguments in favor of Christ. A lot of historical evidence for Jesus' being the Son of God can be investigated using techniques that an investigative journalist would use in pursuing an important news story.

Q: **What kind of feedback have you had from non-Christians?**

One scholar I interviewed told me that we're living in a postmodern world where nobody is interested in the historical evidence for Jesus. But within a short time after the book was published a young person in Mississippi wrote a review online. He had been an atheist, but he read the book and now he's a follower of Christ. Hundreds of people have contacted me saying they have found faith in Christ because the Holy Spirit used this book to help them. One agnostic guy in Chicago was in a bookstore and he sat down to look at a magazine and sat on my book. He started flipping through it, then threw the book aside. Afterwards he had a strong sense that the book was not there by accident. He bought the book and read it. As a result he became a follower of Jesus.

Q: **Did you anticipate the blistering negative reaction to the book from some quarters?**

The book penetrated the stronghold of atheists, agnostics and skeptics. They have tried to attack it from a variety of angles. But the opposition shows that atheists were forced to take the book seriously. I'm glad they haven't been able to disprove it.

Q: **How has becoming a Christian transformed you?**

I once lived a very immoral, self-centered, self-destructive life. I felt my atheism freed me to pursue personal pleasure despite the cost to others. When I accepted Christ, my values and character began to be changed. When I was an atheist I felt no guilt over helping arrange an abortion for a young woman in college. Back then you could have given me a hundred scientific and moral reasons why abortion was wrong and I wouldn't have listened. Now I understand the evil of abortion because I see it from God's perspective.

Q: **Do you miss journalism?**

I loved the daily fray of journalism in a highly competitive city. But nothing else I have ever done can approach the thrill of helping people meet Jesus personally.

— *John W. Kennedy*

John Tesh
In pursuit of passion

John Tesh used to celebrate Hollywood's stars, lifestyles and movies as host of Entertainment Tonight. *Today, he shares his faith through music and, more importantly, his life. When he walked away from* Entertainment Tonight *to pursue a career as a musician many people thought he was making a devastating career move. Not so. Already he has earned three gold albums, six Emmys and two Grammy nominations. Tesh spoke about his music, faith and career.*

Q: You left *Entertainment Tonight*, a television job that paid seven figures. Was that an easy decision?

It was a very easy decision for me to make. Someone handed me a book while I was on vacation that had a list you filled out to pinpoint what you loved and disliked about your job. It was a passion test and I failed it miserably regarding my job on *Entertainment Tonight*. In fact, I got an F. But I got an A-plus when it came to music, so I decided to follow my heart and became a full-time musician.

Q: Musically you've been tagged as everything from New Age musician to worship leader. How do you respond to the New Age label?

I loathe answering those accusations because as Christians they shouldn't be judging me. But I feel like I need to say something so it doesn't appear that I am trying to hide something. There are different categories in the music stores, so when you play mostly instrumental music many stores put your records in the New Age section. I am a Christian who happens to play the piano. I've even asked stores to take my albums out of the New Age bins but they've told us they won't move us because that is where people know where to find us.

Q: You quit *ET*; any other risks you wish you had taken earlier?

I'd risk getting into a stronger relationship with God sooner and I'd risk having more kids and spending more time with them.

Q: What would you say is your greatest gift?

Being average. *[Laughing]* And I was hideously thin and unattractive in high school, which was a blessing in many ways. My grades were average. I hit the honor roll every now and then, but I also got a couple D's. But that kind of beginning makes you work harder. Being known as a stick with a big head and a trumpet in hand humbled me and made me work really hard.

Q: It's strange you call yourself average. In the world's eyes you've done extraordinary things.

Anything extraordinary I've done has not been on my own. Because of my average abilities, the things that have happened with my career have to be supernatural. When I started in broadcasting I'd be in a job for six months and then a job twice as good would come along. This is one reason it is so easy for me to share my faith now, because what has happened in my career can't be explained away as a lucky break.

Q: You grew up in a religious home, but walked away from your faith. Can you tell us about that?

By the time I was 18 I felt I had been over-churched. As a kid I spent four days a week in church. When I went to college in the '60s and everything was a mess, I did things I had never done before. But I can never recall a night when I missed an opportunity to pray. I developed that discipline early on as a child, so there was always a prayer coming out of my mouth. Even though I had strayed from God, He was still connected to me. He was always with me, waiting for me to return.

Q: Let's talk about the day you committed your life to Christ.

I was confirmed as a teen in the Methodist church. I said all the prayers and committed my life to Christ. I had all the Scriptures memorized and I went to church camp every summer and I was committed. But I was only committed to a level that worked for me.

Fast forward to when I met my wife 12 years ago and I entered her church and recommitted my life to Christ and was baptized in the Pacific Ocean a short time later. It was then that I totally committed my life to Christ and was reborn.

Q: What do you value most in life?

I have finally gotten to a place where my connection with God is vital. I have God on the telephone and everything else is on call-waiting. Beyond that it is, of course, my family. I am 51 and I have a 9-year-old daughter and 22-year-old stepson. I am at an age where I have no problem dropping everything and hanging out with them. If I were younger I would probably mess everything up.

Q: **What lesson has your daughter taught you?**

That I need to be present. She just wants me to be in her company. I always want to do something, but she has taught me that kids just want you there. It's like our relationship with God — we just want to know He'll always be there.

Q: **Is it easy to be a believer in Hollywood these days?**

It's easy for me because I am not waiting for a job. I am playing worship music and doing a radio show where the mantra is, "If a 9-year-old can't listen to it, you won't hear it on our show." But what I have learned is that if you share your faith, no matter if you're in Hollywood or Des Moines, be prepared to be attacked.

Q: **Leading people into worship has really got hold of you — how so?**

The difference between worship and other stuff I've done is that it is useful. When I released *Red Rocks, Grand Passion* and *Avalon,* people would e-mail me once and say, *I enjoyed listening to it while I worked around the house.* Now I get e-mails with people saying things like, *My friend listened to the worship album and came to know Christ* or *I found healing from the death of a relative after I listened to such and such song.* It's powerful to be a part of something that is useful. That's really what I want to be: useful.

Q: **What does the future hold for you?**

Who knows? But probably more of the same. I really enjoy finding unusual ways to be a roaring lamb. I live by Bob Briner's book *Roaring Lambs.* I've had opportunities to go onto many television shows and share my faith. It's great how God has allowed me to do that.

— *Kirk Noonan*

Cal Thomas
Finding a mission field

Cal Thomas has become the world's most widely syndicated columnist, appearing in more than 500 newspapers. As a conservative Christian columnist, he has little company in a profession dominated by liberal commentators.

Q: **How do you perceive your work?**

There was a time in my life when I saw the career as an end, supplying not only my physical needs but also my emotional wants. In the process of living and becoming a disciple of Jesus, I found that, like so many other things with God, our ways are not His ways, and my perception has turned around. Now I see career as the means and the credibility it gives me to share my faith among my colleagues in the news industry and also the entertainment industry. It is providing more contentment than I ever had when I was pursuing the elusive goals that the world offers.

Q: **How can laypeople be saltlike Christians in the workplace, wherever they are?**

God wants us to be obedient and He will take care of the results. That's the great mystery of the movement of the Holy Spirit. I think we approach the gospel with an agenda. People only get saved through the work of the Holy Spirit in the individual heart, through the shed blood and finished work of Jesus Christ on the cross. There are lots of people hawking all kinds of religious wares and people can hear a different gospel on every street corner. What they ought to see is how it works out in our lives. Do we stay married? Are we an example to our children? Are we honest in our financial dealings? Do we humble ourselves?

We need a new definition of what the mission field is and what full-time Christian service is. Every believer ought to see him- or herself as in full-time Christian service. The phrase implies there is an alternative — part-time, which is clearly unbiblical. The mission field is wherever God is calling you, in medicine, law, education, the media.

Q: How are you able to balance being truthful with biblical themes, but still be on the cutting edge without being judgmental?

It's very hard, because I'm called upon to make judgments. I'm a columnist; I write opinion pieces. That's what pluralism and the First Amendment are all about; we each get to have our say. Scripture says all have sinned and fall short of the glory of God. But there is a difference in being judgmental and judgment. But I can comment freely, as a believer and as a commentator, and make judgments without being in violation of scriptural mandates.

Q: Any other advice?

A lot of believers don't know Scripture. A lot of Protestant believers, especially, have allowed certain Christian leaders to tell them what the Bible says about redeeming America. So when another believer raises the possibility that this supernationalism may be an incorrect interpretation, they won't look it up for themselves. Go read what God has to say about nations and leaders. You're allowing history to be reinterpreted according to a particular leader who needs you to send him money because you think he's going to fix what's wrong with America. No human, fallen leader is going to save this country. Only Jesus Christ saves individuals. If America became a totalitarian state tomorrow it would not change one thing that I am commanded to do. We've equated money and power and bigness and greatness with the blessing of God.

— *John W. Kennedy*

Kathy Troccoli
A message of hope

Kathy Troccoli's 20-plus years in the Christian music industry have seen their share of ups and downs. Dove Awards, Grammy nominations, television appearances and No. 1 hits have been the highlights; but they've been tempered by losing both parents to cancer, a 10-year struggle with bulimia and a battle with depression. So when this singer-turned-author-turned-speaker tells audiences of women that God will help them through the dark valleys of life, she knows what she's talking about. Troccoli shared how the Lord has given her a message of hope.

Q: **You seem to be concentrating your career on speaking engagements rather than singing these days. Why the change in focus?**

The transitions my career has taken have been remarkable for me. I've sung most of my life and now I feel like I'm finally stepping into my stride of what God has intended for me. I'm speaking a ton now and writing books. My singing is almost the cherry on the cake now, which is very, very new for me. I love that God has taken me through so many seasons in my career so that when I got to this point I'd go, "Ahh, here it is. This is what I've been waiting for." When you have a gift, sometimes you're kind of thrown out there and you go through all these questions. Should I do this? Should I sing this? Should I be here? It wasn't until I turned 40 that I went, "Oh, OK, I get it. You gave me a singing voice, but that's not the main thing. You want me to speak about You and use the singing as an added extra."

Q: What's your message to women?

I don't really consider myself a teacher. I feel more motivational. I have a passion and fire inside of me to ignite women in their faith and remind them of who they are and to whom they belong. So I think my message in all my books and songs and speaking engagements is about hope: You're going to make it. You're going to get through this. God loves you. You're going to be OK.

Q: The difficulties you've overcome seem to have given you credibility.

It's funny you mention that because when I speak I start by saying, "I met the Lord in 1978 and everything has been perfect since." Then I pause and hear this great hush. And I say, "Of course not. We still have suffering as Christians. It's just that our suffering is not in vain." So I give them this list — lost my parents to cancer, went through a struggle with an eating disorder, went through a time of depression — and I begin to see in every woman's eyes this ray of hope because they're thinking, *Wow. Kathy Troccoli has gone through this? And she's making it. She's OK.*

I couldn't offer women what I do now at 45 when I was 25. I didn't have the life behind me. That's not to say that women who are 25 can't speak; it's just that God has given me a testimony. He's given me a message about His faithfulness. So women are more open to what I have to say.

Q: **What triggered your bulimia?**

I always ate normally growing up. As a matter of fact, I ate a lot and kept a fairly decent weight. I grew up in an Italian family and you're around food all the time; they're just stuffing it in your face. But I went through a time of transition when I went to Berklee Jazz School of Music in Boston right out of high school. I hadn't been away from home before. I had never experienced a lot of different philosophies or cultures. And here I was thrown into this jazz school, not a traditional college. Everything was so different. I started questioning what life was about, what am I here for? And before I knew it food became a comfort, and then it turned into an addiction. I saw myself gaining weight like I never had before. I never purged, but I started to abuse laxatives.

Q: **How did you learn to do that?**

It's not like anybody told me how to do it. I just discovered it on my own and found out later that many women abuse laxatives for the same reason — to feel like they're getting rid of it, to feel like they're in control. It happened slowly and became a problem for 10 years.

Q: **Did it develop into anorexia?**

I had a little bout of just not eating, or eating just rice cakes and green beans. I went down, down, down in my weight. You can be bulimic and hold a steady weight; but with the anorexic thinking you really decide that you look heavy and you just quit eating.

Q: **What made you finally seek help?**

I had a roommate who would see me suffer from terrible stomach pains. And one day she said, "You are just ruining yourself." There was swollenness to my appearance because of the toxins in my body. The laxatives become very toxic. I was miserable. I felt like the light was starting to go on then.

So I got to the end of myself and said I really needed help. My roommate helped me get into counseling.

Q: Do you recommend counseling for others struggling with an eating disorder?

Women tend to want a magic wand when dealing with addiction. But it's a process. I really believe in counseling. Bringing things to light. Getting down and digging into things you've held in your soul and your gut and letting God's light shine upon them. It takes time.

Q: Do you still struggle with it?

I can say I am completely delivered from that addiction. I don't have that habit of binging anymore. I have a tendency toward food addiction in the sense that I watch myself closely. I make deliberate choices every day. If I eat a little bit more one day I watch it the next day. I'm always aware that I could fall into bad eating patterns.

Q: What would you say to women who are secretly battling an eating disorder?

You've got to get it in the light. The first step is admitting it. That may be to a mother or close friend, a minister or a counselor. If you keep things in the dark, God's light can't get to it. You have the choice to choose His light or remain in darkness every day. So get it out in the light.

Q: What do you think keeps women from getting help when they're surrounded by people who would gladly help them?

I think there's fear of being known in that way. It's pride, shame or guilt. Or there's denial. And sometimes women just become hopeless. They feel they're stuck in this pattern and God can't possibly be with them.

What I like to do is remind people that God has promised abundant life for the soul. He wants to take you to higher places. You can get out of it. But there is some work to be done. I have rarely seen people in addictions — it doesn't have to be anorexia or bulimia — just get out of them. Yes, God can do the miraculous, but it is usually a process and you have to be committed to the process.

Q: Let's talk about your career. What's your favorite Kathy Troccoli song?

I don't have a particular favorite. I think I'm like anyone who may listen to my music — on any given day I like a certain song better because it just feeds what I need to be fed with. But one in particular would be "A Baby's Prayer." That has absolutely ministered to women who have had abortions or considered having abortions. I have held babies who were not aborted because of that song. I'm just amazed at the power of music.

Q: Is there another artist or song that ministers to you?

Sara Groves is my favorite artist right now. I've been in Christian music for such a long time now, and I am absolutely blown away by Sara's ability to be so poetic, and yet the melodies are so beautiful. Sometimes when you have poets, their songs are unrelatable. The way she puts things is so real and so profound. She has affected my life in the last two years deeply.

Q: After 20 years, three Grammy nominations and countless Dove Awards … what if it all ended today?

I've thought about that because I'm halfway through life. I would be so thankful for the opportunity to continue using the gifts I have in the way I have been using them. If it all ended, there would be an element of missing my singing; but I don't believe it would stop me from wanting to be about Kingdom work. There will always be a person to reach out to. There will always be people in need. There will always be a chance to give life as long as I have life.

Q: **How have your mainstream hits impacted your career?**

It was an interesting time 10 years ago when "Everything Changes" came out. I got to do a lot of TV shows and meet a lot of stars. I think the biggest impact is that I learned more about what it is I should be doing.

Q: **One last question — how tall are you? When I've seen you in concert I see this little person with the biggest voice I've ever heard.**

I'm 5'5" [laughing]. People say that all the time.

— *Ashli O'Connell*

Phil Vischer
The Big Idea behind VeggieTales

Phil Vischer is president and "top tomato" of Big Idea Productions, best known for the popular, computer-animated VeggieTales *children's video series. Vischer started Big Idea in 1993 in a spare bedroom in his home. Today, the family-entertainment company has sold more than 20 million videos promoting "Sunday morning values, Saturday morning fun." Vischer writes many of the* VeggieTales *stories and songs, and is the voice of a number of characters, including Bob the Tomato.*

 What is the purpose of Big Idea?

Our mission is to markedly enhance the moral and spiritual fabric of our culture through creative media — to make the lessons and values of the Bible relevant to our generation. We believe that popular media (TV, movies, music, etc.), used irresponsibly, have had a profoundly negative impact on spiritual and moral health in our culture. We also believe, however, that the same media, used well, could have an equally positive impact.

Q: How aware are most parents about the media's influence on their children?

Parental awareness varies. The folks who make *Sesame Street* commissioned a study that found parents fall into three primary groups: protective, progressive and indifferent. Protective parents view media — and the world in general — as a dangerous influence that can rob their kids of their innocence. They try to protect their kids from these influences, screening media carefully.

Progressive parents feel that the world is full of great possibilities for their kids. They search out new, progressive media options and encourage their kids to jump in with both feet.

The group labeled "indifferent" tends not to take an active role in either guiding their kids away from or toward particular media. This is the group most likely to underestimate the impact media is having on their kids.

Many Christian parents fall into the "protective" group but will often exhibit some of the characteristics of the "progressive" parents, seeking out media to actively engage the emotional and moral development of their kids.

Q: How can parents create a safe media environment for their children?

Monitor your kids' media consumption as closely as you monitor their food consumption. What they put in their minds will affect them at least as much as what they put in their mouths. Steer them away from negative options; but as often as possible, explain your reasoning. The ultimate goal is to raise a child who can make healthy media choices. A child needs to learn to discern, not simply be told what he or she can and cannot watch. I really believe that parents should keep media devices (TVs, VCRs, computers with Internet access) in public areas (living rooms or studies).

This one is a biggie: Make kids' rooms media-free zones. No TVs. No Internet access. Giving kids freedom to view whatever they want in their own rooms is the equivalent of letting them eat, drink or smoke whatever they want in their own rooms. The goal is to send our kids into the world with the skills to make good choices. If we think they can do that at the age of 12, we're sorely mistaken.

Q: What criteria do you use in selecting what television and videos your own children may watch?

First, we look for "absence of bad." Do the characters portray behavior or promote values we wouldn't want to see in our kids? In other words, will this show make it harder for me to raise healthy, godly kids? Then, we look for "presence of good." Is this a show our kids could actually learn from? Quite often, the best we can get from Hollywood is the "absence of bad."

We want parents to know that with anything from Big Idea, not only will there always be an "absence of bad," but we will always add in heaping spoonfuls of "presence of good."

Q: What can Christians do to help undo the negative effects of exposure to mainstream media?

We absolutely need to teach our kids to think critically. If they can't consider a statement presented by a likable character on TV or in a movie and say, "That isn't true," they will have a very hard time living on their own in a media-drenched culture. A huge part of parenting is modeling that kind of critical thinking.

We also need to steer our kids toward positive media choices. They need to see the difference between "good" and "bad."

Q: What do you think about isolating kids completely from non-Christian media?

There are several things that concern me about this tactic: First, the purpose of parenting is to teach our kids how to make good choices, so they can eventually leave home and live successfully on their own. If they're presented with nothing but Christian media choices growing up, we may find them unable to deal with the real world when they leave home — not unlike a kid who grows up knowing nothing but health food, then goes off to school and finds himself in the junk food aisle at the supermarket. Is he prepared to handle his new options?

My greater concern, however, is sending our kids the message that the only valid artistic or creative expression is an overtly Christian expression. Thus, if God has blessed our kids with creative talent, they will very likely feel that they are misusing their talent unless every song or story they write deals with explicit Christian themes. This dynamic, in a very real way, has greatly reduced the impact of Christian artists on our culture.

Like much of life, media isn't necessarily a black or white affair. My family's choices won't necessarily look like the family down the block, or even the family next to me at church. What's important is that I've established clear principles to help us make choices; that I enforce them consistently, fairly and with explanation; and that, as my kids grow, they are given more and more opportunities to apply those principles themselves.

Q: How has Hollywood responded to VeggieTales?

The reactions have varied from "This is really cool!" to "Hmm ... I don't get it." Many of the folks in the industry that we've spoken to love the humor and the production value, but are a bit perplexed by the references to God and the Bible. "Why would you do that? Nobody wants God in their entertainment!"

When they find out how popular *VeggieTales* has become, they go from perplexed to downright befuddled.

Q: As the popularity of *VeggieTales* grows, has there been pressure to compromise the Christian message?

Oh, there was pressure almost from Day 1. In 1995, we had offers to take us into mass market stores — as long as we edited God out of the videos. We declined, which was a pretty hard call since we were having trouble meeting payroll that year.

The next year, others said we could leave God in, as long as we took the Bible verses out. Again, we declined.

It wasn't until 1998 that we found a distributor who was willing to take *VeggieTales* into mass market stores as is. So we've gotten used to the pressure.

Overall, lots of folks would love to work with us (including major networks) if we'd just stick to warm, fuzzy life lessons. Everybody loves a good life lesson. But we don't want to teach kids to forgive just because it makes the world a nicer place; we want to teach kids to forgive because, when they do something wrong, God is always ready to forgive them. The lesson we're teaching is not ultimately about forgiveness; it is about God. We have walked away from many opportunities and will continue to do so, to stay true to our mission.

Q: **Talk about your long-term plans for Big Idea Productions.**

The world is now dominated by just a handful of giant, global media companies. These companies influence values and beliefs on a global scale. Much more so than any preacher or politician.

Our vision is to build a media company that is driven not by profit motive, but rather by the desire to help people rediscover the lessons and values of the Bible. Wherever people are watching movies and TV shows, buying videos or listening to music, we want to be there offering them options that will improve their lives, not just take their money.

— *Ashli O'Connell*

Lisa Whelchel
An advocate for moms

Lisa Whelchel, a star of the 1980s television series Facts of Life, *started MomTime, a ministry for moms, more than 10 years ago. MomTime can be accessed at LisaWhelchel.com. Whelchel spoke about her passion for moms and families.*

Q: Why did you start a ministry for moms?

It was an outgrowth of my life. I filmed the last episode of *Facts of Life* in March 1988 and was married that July. Steve and I started our family soon after we got married, and within the next three years we had three children. I found myself in suburbia with three kids in diapers. I was lonely for adult conversation and interaction, so I put together the first MomTime group.

Q: What's a MomTime group?

It's one day in the week where moms can laugh, cry, talk, eat and have fun with other moms. The gathering is a time for moms to take for themselves because they usually put themselves at the bottom of the priority list. It's about refueling and refreshing so moms can give and give again for another week.

Q: Why are relationships with other moms so important?

It's biblical to talk with other moms and glean practical wisdom from each other. We live in such a spread out, disconnected, fast-paced world that it takes time to build relationships. Moms have to be intentional about making and fostering relationships because when the hard times come they need a supportive infrastructure in place.

Q: Should moms work or stay at home?

The ideal situation is for moms to be home with their children. But I know we don't live in an ideal world. There are circumstances where a mom would love to be home, but can't. For me it's ideal to be a stay-at-home mom and homeschool my children, but I don't think it's God's written law that we do either.

Q: Does your ministry take you away from home?

Sometimes it takes me away from my husband, kids and home way more than I want and way more than it should, but I also know that I would be disobeying the Lord if I did not do this ministry.

Q: What advice would you give dads?

In some homes it's as if Mom and the kids speak a different language than Dad. But the common denominators in the most successful families I know are dads who are intentionally and actively involved in the lives of their wife and kids.

Q: What encouragement would you give to moms?

Moms need to know they are not alone. Some moms feel like they yell too much or that their kids' attitudes are stinky or that their house is a mess. Many moms feel like failures.

Q: How can moms deal with those feelings?

It should move a mom to pray for her children. Whenever that feeling of failure comes, moms should start praying. When we turn ourselves and our children over to God, good things happen. It's only when God touches a mom's heart that it will be changed.

Q: What's the best thing a mom can do for her children?

Pray and consecrate them to the hands of the Lord. He will train and keep them even beyond 18 years of age.

— *Kirk Noonan*

Philip Yancey
Understanding grace

Philip Yancey is known for insight, sensitivity and candor in his award-winning books. He is editor-at-large for Christianity Today, *and author of* The Jesus I Never Knew *and* What's So Amazing About Grace?, *among other titles.*

Q: What draws you to the subjects you write about?

I'm spiraling closer to the center of faith. When I started writing I was on the margins, which is why I chose the tough problems: pain, disappointment, unanswered prayer. Now I am more confident dealing with what faith is all about, which is why the book on Jesus was such a huge step. It was important to ask who this Person was whom I spent my life following.

It was my study of Jesus that brought me to *What's So Amazing About Grace?* I found that the qualities that defined His life were not always the qualities that come to mind when people think of Christians. I wondered what we were doing differently from Jesus.

Q: **You write that many preach grace, but practice ungrace. How do you think that came about?**

It happened in Jesus' day. There was no group He was harsher toward than the Pharisees. As I look at the history of the Church, I see a pattern: We are called to proclaim God's love for sinners. That's why the gospel is good news. But we turn it into a system of morality.

We are called to be holy and moral; but as soon as you make your primary emphasis a spiritual ranking system, you define insiders and outsiders and become concerned with society's morals instead of your own dependence on God and His forgiveness of you. It's a built-in temptation born of pride. You can see it in our glimpses of the Early Church. A clear example of ungrace is when Paul stood down Peter for not eating with the Gentiles. All the apostles had to fight the ungrace of the Jewish Christians being superior to the Gentile Christians.

Q: **Why is grace so difficult?**

Grace sounds great in the abstract, but not in the practical. Tolstoy's line, paraphrased, is, "The more I love humanity in general, the harder I find it to love individuals." It's easy to say, "Love your enemy. What a sweet concept Jesus came up with." But when you actually have an enemy out there, to show love is difficult. The heart gets involved and you realize how tough grace is. It goes against nature. But, like the ungrateful servant, we need to spend our time remembering the mountain of sin that the Father has forgiven us; and that no matter what anybody on earth does to us, it's petty by contrast. That's what motivates us to treat others how we want to be treated. The Lord's Prayer invites God to forgive us as we forgive others, which is a terrifying thing to ask.

Q: **How does grace fit into society?**

I am concerned that in America a lot of Christians' attention goes to societal issues, which are important. But when I look at the space the New Testament devotes to issues of the day, there's not much.

Wouldn't it be a tragedy if the conservative church repeated the error of the liberal church in the 1960s, which was preaching politics, not the gospel? People left in droves. If people keep coming to conservative churches and hearing political messages, even ones they agree with, we could be in trouble. People come to church to meet God. We are not called to create a moral society, but to proclaim God's love for sinners, which transforms people from the inside out.

Q: **At one point you were training to be a missionary. Do you feel like a "missionary" with your books?**

In some ways, but it's a vicarious work. I get letters years after I have struggled with a certain subject. The word is a quiet way of communicating the gospel, easy to reject. My own faith has been formed by the written word. I have faith that what I'm doing will have a similar effect on someone else.

Q: **Is there anything that concerns you about the evangelical church?**

Yes — how small a role Christians allow the local church to play in their lives. For many people, Sunday morning is their one spiritual shot all week. It's been narrowed down to an hour a week, and that's not enough. People treat it as a duty they accomplish before they do whatever they want — one more item on the consumer's agenda. That's a long way from, "Take up [your] cross and follow me" (Matthew 16:24).

— *Joel Kilpatrick*

Darlene Zschech
Sing, shout . . . just praise the Lord

Darlene Zschech is worship pastor at Hillsong Church in Sydney, Australia. She has been nominated for a handful of Dove Awards and is the writer of the popular worship song "Shout to the Lord," which was nominated for Song of the Year for the 1998 Dove Awards.

Q: **How did you come to lead worship?**

I didn't want to be a worship leader. I love being in the background arranging, recording and producing. But one Sunday Pastor Brian Houston was leading worship and he just walked off and left me in the middle of the service. At the time I was just not confident enough to lead worship. I think in my heart I just needed that bit of confidence of Brian turning the worship over to me.

Q: **How has being in the spotlight challenged you?**

I take that very seriously. The spotlight doesn't give you much room for error, that's for sure. No one's perfect. I've made a lot of mistakes. I've got a lot of mistakes yet to make

— we all do. I try to love my team, church and family. The rest is just doing whatever I can do to the best of my ability.

Q: **In your book *Extravagant Worship*, you say you want to make God's name famous. What do you mean by that?**

Australian culture is very secular. There's no generational understanding of who God is and why you would want to make Him the center of your life. So from that point of view, we want to really exalt the name of Christ in our nation and so become Christ-centered.

Q: **How do you relate personally to the people you work with?**

All of the people who work for Mark and me are in our cell group, which really helps. We've done that on purpose. So every week there are a few outlets. The cell is sort of like our family, so we can pray for things and it's really good. We've been there for a long time. So they've seen the good, the bad, and the ugly. We don't just pray together or do church together; we do life together.

Q: **Why is it important for worship leaders to pass their knowledge of worship onto others?**

I would like to be a worship leader forever, but more and more I try to give it away and raise up more people to become involved. Some of what I've learned — it's not all perfect — I want to share, because if I can save someone from having to go through some of the potholes that I have hit, then praise God. I think there are many Scriptures in the Bible that make it clear that our responsibility as Christian leaders is to not hold anything back.

Q: **What's your take on the popularity and commercial success of worship and how it is used?**

I think we're going to have to deal with a lot more of success. Christian music should be on the radio and on the mainstream airways. It's not just for the church. It has the ability to draw people to the church because God's presence is attached to it. It's so inviting for the hungry heart of humanity.

Q: Do you find that there are times when you feel inadequate?

Yes, each day. I think that's what makes it great. All our team feels like that. That gap between what it is you're feeling in your heart and what is real is so big that it has to be God at work. So it sort of keeps you swimming in the miraculous, because without Him we can do nothing.

Q: In your latest book, *The Kiss of Heaven*, you talk of a life of favor ... about empowering a life dream.

I believe God's promise, that if you seek His righteousness, peace and joy in the Holy Spirit that God desires to give you above and beyond everything you need to accomplish your purpose on earth. I think that seeking God's favor in our lives is not selfish if we understand the reason it is given. Not to be hoarded, but with open hands to give. We are not favored for ourselves. We are blessed to bless others. I believe that is why we have His favor.

Q: What would you say to those who desire His favor?

Delight God's heart by serving Him. Do well with whatever is in your hand today. I think you will sense His smile as you desire to love and serve Him above all else.

— *Keith Locke*

About the
interviewers

James Bilton is former promotions coordinator for *Today's Pentecostal Evangel.* He is now a businessman in the Kansas City area.

Belinda Conway is former permissions and information coordinator for *Today's Pentecostal Evangel.* She is now a support specialist for Assemblies of God World Missions.

Paul Cossentine is former staff writer for North Central University (Assemblies of God) in Minneapolis, Minn.

Hal Donaldson is editor in chief of *Today's Pentecostal Evangel* and president and CEO of Convoy of Hope.

Ann Floyd is former associate editor of *Today's Pentecostal Evangel.* She is now retired and living in Springfield, Mo.

Scott Harrup is associate editor of *Today's Pentecostal Evangel.*

Ken Horn is managing editor of *Today's Pentecostal Evangel.*

John W. Kennedy is news editor of *Today's Pentecostal Evangel.*

Joel Kilpatrick is former associate editor of *Today's Pentecostal Evangel.* He is now a freelance writer living in Los Angeles, Calif.

Ron Kopczick is promotions coordinator for *Today's Pentecostal Evangel.*

Keith Locke is former creative director for *Today's Pentecostal Evangel.* He is now a freelance designer living in Springfield, Mo.

John Maempa is former managing editor of *Today's Pentecostal Evangel.* He is currently editor in chief of Radiant Life Resources.

Kirk Noonan is associate editor of *Today's Pentecostal Evangel.*

Ashli O'Connell is assistant editor of *Today's Pentecostal Evangel.*

Don Spradling is pastor of Christian Life Church (Assemblies of God) in Long Beach, Calif.

Amber Weigand-Buckley is editor of *On Course* magazine, an Assemblies of God youth publication.

Matt Wilkie is an Assemblies of God missionary with Book of Hope.

Gail Wood is a freelance writer living in Lacey, Wash.

Need to order more copies from the Pentecostal Evangel Books library?

Q&A: Conversations with 50 inspiring people
GPH #02-3031   ISBN 0-88243-325-3

The Write Way: A believer's guide
to effective communication
GPH #02-3034   ISBN 0-88243-693-7

50 Tough Questions
GPH #02-3033   ISBN 0-88243-343-1

Questions and Answers about the Holy Spirit
GPH #02-3032   ISBN 0-88243-303-2

Family: How to have a healthy Christian home
GPH #02-1034   ISBN 0-88243-342-3

To purchase any of the above titles,
or for more information,
call Gospel Publishing House at
1-800-641-4310.
Or visit: www.gospelpublishing.com

Want more inspirational conversations?

Enjoy a new interview every week
when you subscribe to
Today's Pentecostal Evangel.

To subscribe or for more
information, please call 1-800-641-4310
or visit www.pe.ag.org.

Discounted bundle subscriptions of six or more copies
to one address are also available.